CLASSICAL LIVING

CLASSICAL LIVING

Reconnecting with the Rituals of Ancient Rome

*Myths, Gods, Goddesses, Celebrations,
and Rites for Every Month of the Year*

Frances Bernstein, Ph.D.

HarperSanFrancisco
A Division of HarperCollinsPublishers

HarperCollins books may be purchased for educational, business, or sales promotional use. For information please write: Special Markets Department, HarperCollins Publishers Inc., 10 East 53rd Street, New York, NY 10022.

HarperCollins Web site: http://www.harpercollins.com

HarperCollins®, 📖®, and HarperSanFrancisco™ are trademarks of HarperCollins Publishers Inc.

FIRST EDITION

Designed by Lindgren/Fuller Design

Illustrations by Kathleen Edwards

Library of Congress Cataloging-in-Publication Data
Bernstein, Frances.
    Classical living : reconnecting with the rituals of ancient Rome / Frances Bernstein.
        p. cm.
    Includes index.
    ISBN 0–06–251624–8 (cloth)
    ISBN 0–06–251625–6 (pbk.)
    1. Rites and ceremonies—Rome. 2. Religious calendars—Rome. 3. Rome—Religion.
    4. Rome—Religious life and customs. 5. Spiritual life. I. Title.
    BL808.B47 2000
    292.3'8—dc21   99–055433

00 01 02 03 04 ❖/RRD (H) 10 9 8 7 6 5 4 3 2 1

For My Parents

CONTENTS

ACKNOWLEDGMENTS

This book is an integration and expression of the various and meaningful parts of my life: my historical and archaeological research, my personal spiritual journey, and the love of family and friends. I owe my gratitude and acknowledgment to my colleagues, Lorna Cahall, Wilhelmina Jashemski, Betty Jo Mayeske, David Orr, and Michael Reamy, for their advice and support. Thank you also to my agents, Gail Ross and Howard Yoon, and to the editors at HarperSanFrancisco, Liz Perle, David Hennessy, Terri Leonard, and Garrett Brown, for helping shape the manuscript.

My heartfelt thanks is offered to the women who gather with me monthly to create a living, spiritual bond: Dorothy Britt, Marney Bruce, Jamie Burnett, Helen Cannon, Helen Poponoe, Kay Quam, and Sheryl Schultz. Their ideas, suggestions, and enthusiasm for this project were invaluable.

I could have never written *Classical Living* without the unwavering support, patience, and love of my dear family: my daughter, Rachel; my son, Aaron; and my husband, Roger. Thank you always!

INTRODUCTION

A BRIDGE FROM THE PAST

My team of archaeologists worked long summer days inside the homes of ancient Pompeians. We measured, photographed, and recorded the colorful mythic scenes painted on the walls. We did not expect that these powerful archetypal images of gods and goddesses, nymphs and heroes, birds, dogs, snakes, flowers, trees, labyrinths, or rituals would trigger dreams. We came to realize that these symbols painted over 2,000 years ago comprised a living language, and to our amazement, we had incorporated these sacred images in our own dreams. Our deeply personal responses to these ancient symbols formed a bridge and a sacred connection spanning two millennia.

I cannot take each of you to Pompei. Yet the classical myths and rituals presented in these pages can awaken a deep and ancient connection to the natural world and our spirituality. Dreamlike images of creation, life, and death work on many levels and transcend time. The realm of gods and goddesses is not limited to a prehistoric period or to ancient Rome, but resides within nature and the cycle of birth, life, and death. By tapping into this deeper realm, we touch the underlying and true universals that connect us to the world and guide us in our daily lives.

> I am telling you the truth, but some will say that I made it up because most people doubt the existence of the deities and the spirits. A god, a goddess resides within each of us. When the spirit arouses us, we radiate with an inner glow— an aura. It is this sacred spirit that plants the seeds of all we are and all we do. This sacred spirit is our inspiration.
>
> (Ovid *Fasti* 6.3)

We journey back to a time when people communed with nature through poetry, myth, and ritual. The sacred calendar of the ancient Romans described an actual pathway for life's journey with the gods and goddesses as spiritual guides. These deities drew the Romans into harmony with nature and grounded all life. The twelve months charted the path of sacred time by following the never-ending cycle of birth, growth, fullness, death, and rebirth. Ancient practices based upon rhythms of the natural world can strengthen and heal. This earthy ancient lore serves as a guide today, as we search for relevance and meaning in lives that are increasingly cut off from nature and the life of the inner self.

We draw on rituals that were practiced in antiquity for thousands of years in order to trigger intense and deeply personal spiritual and emotional responses. The ancient Romans have given us, through their sacred calendar, a way to live with the mysteries of the natural world. We can come to understand the sacred message—a message that is limitless, omnipresent, and accessible to those who seek it.

ROMAN RELIGION

Religious life in ancient Rome, composed of diverse cults, philosophical schools, and mystery rites, was both rich and complex, spanning a period of over a thousand years. In Rome, there was a temple on almost every corner, some of early origin and others built with the riches of the empire. Many of the rituals presented in this book harken back to the early days of the city, yet some rites were transposed and adapted from the Near East or Egypt. All are authentic; all were once practiced, and therein lies their power.

The great city of Rome was founded in the early centuries of the first millennium B.C.E. (before the common era) by Latin-speaking farmers and shepherds living on the hilltops along the banks of the Tiber River. As Rome grew in size and importance, the Latin people fell under the religious influence of the Etruscans, who lived to the north, and the Greeks, who settled southern Italy during the seventh and sixth centuries B.C.E. and whose deities, rites, and mythology were blended with the more traditional Roman worship. Later, as the Roman Empire expanded into foreign lands, religions from Egypt and the Near East had an impact upon Roman religion. Christianity was one such form of worship from the Near East.

Roman religion was experienced through myth and ritual. The Roman gods and goddesses portrayed in the myths were also honored publicly at temples through prayer, rituals, and offerings that might include the gift of an animal, food, wine, or a small votive such as a clay image. Privately, the deities and spirits were worshiped within each and every Roman household before the household shrines.

THE HOME AS A SACRED CENTER

In ancient Rome, the home and family grounded religious belief and observance. Then, as now, the women often provided spiritual guidance by marking the religious calendar with yearly observances, passing on religious teachings, and creating a sacred sanctuary within the home.

The Romans worshiped before family shrines, called *lararia*. In the Roman world, the home was a spiritual center and in most ancient times the hearth was the first altar. The hearth goddess Vesta was especially sacred to the Romans; her beneficence meant good fortune would fall on the household. Vesta's presence and protective powers were embodied in the living flame of every family's hearth. At her main shrine in Rome, attended by six Vestal Virgins, there was no cult statue because the Romans believed that Vesta herself was the "Living Flame."

The entrance hall, atrium, kitchen, and garden, focal points within the ancient Roman home, were the most common locations for a *lararium*. Homes often had more than one shrine set up for family rituals. Types of lararia varied from a niche within a wall (the most common) to a miniature temple façade, a separate small building, or just a sacred scene painted

> ### PRAYER TO VESTA
>
> Come, Vesta, to live in the Beautiful Home.
> Come with warm feelings of friendship.
> Bring your intelligence,
> Your Energy and your Passion
> To join with your Good Work.
> Burn always in my Soul.
> You are welcome here.
> I remember You.

3

on a wall. All household shrines had in common some provision for making sacrifice, either a ledge or altar. Altars could be large permanent ones placed before a shrine or much smaller portable ones set up before a sacred painting. Often a depiction of an altar with burning sacrifice and offerings was painted on the wall next to the sacred scene as permanent testimony.

Women tended these family shrines, cleaning and decorating them to ensure family deities were honored properly. By custom, three times a month, on the Kalends (new moon), the Nones, and the Ides (full moon), women decorated the hearth and the shrines with fresh flowers, woven garlands, and wreaths. "In oldest times, the goodwill of the gods and goddesses was won with simple offerings of grain or a few salt crystals. The altar was content to smoke with laurel leaves [bay leaves] crackling in the fire, while the woman who could add a garland of meadow flowers or violets was rich indeed" (Ovid *Fasti* 1.333–45).

The spirits and deities honored within the Roman home included the Penates, the Lares, and the Genius and Juno. The Penates were the guardian forces of the pantry—the ones that protected the food supply. The family Lares, very special guardian spirits, were honored by each family to protect health and welfare. The guiding spirits and procreative forces that ensured continuity of the family were the Genius and the Juno—the male and female spirits of the father and mother, the paterfamilias and materfamilias. The Genius and Juno were worshiped by the family before the household altar on each of the parents' birthdays with an offering of honey cakes and wine. Statuettes of gods and goddesses, the ones very special to the family, were an integral part of the shrine and were placed inside the niches together with personal mementos and offering gifts.

The family would gather together at the shrine for prayer and offering to these spirits and deities. The father or mother, serving as priest or priestess with head veiled, would lead the prayer with palms outstretched facing the sky. A small offering cake or an egg placed on the altar, a bit of incense burned, and a few drops of wine poured into the earth before the shrine comprised the family ritual. The household shrine was a sacred center within private space and hence provided an opportunity for an individual to spend a quiet moment of prayer, offer a special gift, and seek a very personal encounter with the divine.

4

THE SACRED CALENDAR, THE RELIGIOUS YEAR

The varied aspects of Roman religion are marshaled on a month-by-month basis in the Roman sacred calendar, established by the high priest. It is this calendar that charted the rituals and rites to the various deities, noting days of festivals, days for family celebrations, and days to honor the gods and goddesses. This ancient sacred calendar, which once structured the religious life of the Romans, forms the core of this book.

Here, ancestral wisdom of daily religious practice gleaned over thousands of years, passed down from generation to generation, can both instruct and inspire us today as we too seek to twine together the sacred and the mundane. We can return spiritually to an era when people lived in communion with nature through myth and ritual, for the path described by the Roman sacred calendar is more closely connected to the natural world than the path most of us follow today. A religious calendar is different from a secular one, as time is reckoned in a cyclical progression with the religious festivals and rites repeated the same way every year. In the Roman sacred calendar from January to December, we note periods of beginnings, growth, nurturing, ripening, and dying—only to begin again.

The sacred calendar follows the seasons. To live in harmony with this yearly natural cycle meant honoring the deities with rites and rituals appropriate to each season, and it is these rites that make up the sacred calendar. Winter brings the period of birth when sunlight is born again at the winter solstice. The yearly cycle proceeds then through spring, the period of growth; summer, the period of attainment; and autumn, the period of death and endings.

The oldest sacred calendars were all lunar—based not upon the earth's path around the sun, but on the monthly cycle of the moon. Because the ancients saw their year defined by the moon and women's menstrual cycle, the sacred calendar presented here provides both solar and lunar dates for all rituals.

The oldest Roman lunar calendar divided the month into three main focal points: the Kalends, the Nones, and the Ides. The Kalends was the first day after the dark moon, when the high priest watched for the sighting of the thin crescent of light before calling the people together for sacrifice. The Kalends was generally sacred to Juno, wife of Jupiter and Goddess of the Dark Moon. The Nones, the ninth day before the full moon, fell on either the fifth or seventh of the month. On the Nones, the high priest once again called together the people of the village to announce the sacred rites for the remaining days of the month. The Ides was the day of the full moon, an auspicious and very sacred time. Dates were reckoned in number of days before the Kalends, Nones, and Ides; for example, "VIII Kalends March," or "eighth day before the Kalends of March."

Today, close to twenty calendars from the ancient Roman world survive and most date from the first centuries of the common era, after Julius Caesar changed the calendar from a lunar to a solar one in 46 B.C.E. In fact, it is Caesar's calendar, with some modifications, that is our calendar today. As the years passed, additions were made to the calendar to reflect dates of significance in the mighty Roman Empire. The birthdays of the emperors were added as festival days, and the days commemorating battles and conquests were designated for sacrifice. Thus, by the late Empire (the third or fourth centuries C.E.), the solar calendar was a composite based on ancient agricultural rites interspersed with political events and great battles. Another extremely valuable source of information is the *Fasti* by the Roman author Ovid, who lived at the beginning of the common era. This colorful narrative on Roman religion follows the religious year citing ritual and myth related to the monthly cycle.

I want to return to the lunar calendar, which was the true cycle for the original calendar and the oldest festivals and rituals. I have attempted to restore the rites of the most ancient gods and goddesses to their true days in the month. For example, Roman women walked fifteen miles at night from the city of Rome to Diana's sacred lake at Nemi on the Ides, or full moon, of the ninth lunation, or August. The full moon was a time of vibrant female energy. When Caesar made the calendar a solar one, he permanently fixed the Ides on the fifteenth of the month. So Diana's ritual took place every August 13 and not necessarily on the full moon of August. Thus, after Caesar, these poor Roman women had to walk in the dark to honor the goddess on her holy day.

JANUARY: The Month to Begin
FEBRUARY: The Month to Purify
MARCH: The Month to Plant the Seed
APRIL: The Month to Conceive
MAY: The Month to Blossom
JUNE: The Month to Nurture
JULY: The Month to Savor
AUGUST: The Month to Reap
SEPTEMBER: The Month to Harvest Life
OCTOBER: The Month to Promise
NOVEMBER: The Month to Accept
DECEMBER: The Month to Hope

HOW TO USE THIS BOOK

By following the sacred calendar in this book, you will, through the rites and rituals, tap into the ancient lore, reconnecting with the natural cycle and sacred spirit. We follow the yearly calendar, noting the days of the rituals for each month as prescribed in antiquity. Each monthly chapter will follow a similar format featuring an underlying theme, a myth associated with the month, and a listing of the dates and descriptions of the ancient rituals.

In addition, I interpret the meaning of the gods and goddesses of the month, the rituals honoring them, and the ancient myths, while offering insights for spiritual growth and revealing ways to reconnect with the ancient Roman sacred calendar.

Classical Living is meant to be a resource and guide. The modern rituals I suggest are drawn from my experiences; adapt and alter them to fit your needs and beliefs. My purpose is not to be dogmatic, but instead to allow you to experience the ancestral wisdom in your own way. I serve as a *pontifex,* a "bridge builder," offering a pathway to the ancient pagan world. What you carry with you when you return across the bridge is up to you.

JANUARY

THE MONTH TO BEGIN

My house seemed brighter than a moment before.
Then holy Janus, an amazing sight with those two heads,
suddenly met me face to face.
Frightened out of my wits, I felt my hair stand on end
and suddenly an icy chill gripped my heart.
With a staff in his right hand, and a key in his left, the god
uttered these words from his forward mouth:
"I am called Janus the doorman!" (Ovid Fasti 1.97)

Rural Menologia
SUN IN CAPRICORN
31 DAYS
NONES: JANUARY 5
DAYLIGHT: 9 ³/₄ HOURS
DARKNESS: 14 ¹/₄ HOURS

Ancient Roman farmers were advised to refrain from working the soil until mid-month except on January 1, when they were to make a symbolic beginning of work of every type to ensure good luck!

This was a period for cleaning up, repairing tools, and planning for the upcoming year. Jobs that were appropriate for the second half of January included sharpening stakes, cutting reeds and willows, and sacrificing to the Dei Penates, the spirits of the pantry. (Menologia)

The sun and the year start from the same point. (Ovid Fasti *1.164)*

So should we! It is time to begin. January is the month for initiation and for New Year's resolutions. We take stock of the emotional tools we will need, set goals, and plan for new growth. It is the month to make choices and to get going. It is the month to open new doors, to begin.

Beginning something new, whether it is the new year, a different job, a new relationship, or a journey, means transcending a boundary and moving from what is old and familiar to what is new and unknown. These points of new beginning in our lives may reflect the passage of time from one year to the next or involve lifestyle changes. These transitions were sacred moments to the ancient Romans and called for offering and prayer to Janus. It was he who oversaw all beginnings and assured prosperity and success for all new endeavors.

What an amazing sight Janus is with two faces and keys jangling from his belt. The namesake of this first month was a most ancient and complex deity whose origin harkened back to a primordial time—a time before the divine spirits had human form. Janus is all-powerful. He sees our past and looks into our future. No one escapes the piercing vision of the god Janus, as the nymph Cranae learned too well. Here is her story.

Janus and Cranae

There once was a nymph called Cranae who lived in an ancient grove of trees near the Tiber River. She roamed the countryside and chased wild animals with her spear; she set up her rope nets across entire valleys.

She was a wild woman, beautiful and free; some even called her Diana, but she wasn't. Whenever a young man approached her with seductive words, seeking to lie down with her in the warm green meadow, Cranae would always respond with the same words.

"I am too embarrassed, people could see us making love, the light is too bright. Lead me to a cave and I will follow." How easy it is to fool men, she thought, as she hid in some bushes, not to be found.

One day two-faced Janus saw Cranae roaming the hills, and his passion was aroused for this wandering nymph. He used gentle words, trying his best to seduce her. As usual, the nymph told Janus to go ahead and find a secluded cave where the two could meet for lovemaking. He believed her and went on ahead. Pretending to follow, Cranae sought a hiding place. Foolish girl!

Janus can see what happens behind his back, and he knows where people hide. He is not a god to be taken lightly. He got what he wanted from Cranae and in return made her the Goddess of Door Hinges. He gave her a white thorn branch, a magical charm she uses to keep all harm and evil spirits from doorways.

January is a month for honest endeavor, serious planning, and forethought. It is not the time for deception or games, which have severe consequences, as the nymph Cranae discovered. She foolishly tried to deceive Janus, the God of Beginnings

In this myth, the nymph Cranae teaches us from her mistake just how valuable a knowledge of the past is. She thought by tricking all the men who sought her that she was in charge and had power over the situation. And she did, until she met Janus. Cranae underestimated Janus's insightfulness and his ability to look backward.

In this myth, two-faced Janus challenges us to seriously think about time and change, and the complex and risky process of making a deliberate decision to strike out in a new direction. We learn from the God of Beginnings and Thresholds that change is not something we should rush into without reflecting upon where we have been. It is essential that we draw upon our awareness of the past and expectations for the future. This is a critical time when we must be conscious of the past and where we have been, those things we have done or thought, the experiences that are over—lessons learned.

Janus embodies a balanced perspective, something Cranae lacked and for which she paid a price. So, we can learn from the story of Cranae not to rush into a new situation, but to move forward deliberately. Most important, we must not close our eyes to the lessons of the past as we plan for the future.

To make a good decision for the future, we need to draw upon all six senses and sift through past experiences. We must research and learn more, but also trust in intuition and hunches. Although this was an easy task for Janus, who can at see two ways at once, it is a bit trickier for us. Awareness is critical to prevent injury and harm in our future. Nature encourages this thoughtful, contemplative process as well. January is the month to think of beginnings, to plan and prepare.

January is a cold barren month. In many parts of the country, it is the time to seek shelter from falling temperatures, bitter winds, and driving rain or swirling snow outside. Just as the she-bear, driven by an instinct aeons old, is safely curled up in the warmth of a quiet cave, so cozy and content, we also obey nature's dictates and seek the warmth and comfort of family and hearth. On a spiritual level, we must also follow nature's directive as we turn inward, rally our forces, provision ourselves, and hone our tools for success in the upcoming year. We dig in this month, extending roots deep down into the rich dark soil to align ourselves spiritually with the agricultural cycle. The deities that were honored in January and the ancient rituals that were practiced by the Romans this month convey season-bound messages. This is the right time to gently close our eyes and go into dark places, to sleep, to dream, to heal, and to begin. This is the lesson for January.

This month, set aside some time to think deeply about beginnings and opening doors. We should imagine crossing over an unfamiliar threshold and making a change, thinking of what may lie beyond.

There can be many types of beginnings, and although some may appear small or trivial, each is a start-up, the dawn of a new day—each new step your child takes, a different task at work, a new acquaintance. We may set off down an unknown and truly different life path with a new job or a journey to a new place. We must learn to observe the doors that open to us every day, the thresholds that we routinely cross. We will come to recognize and cherish the moments marking something new, however brief they may be. Each and every beginning must be viewed as special, as a magical moment in our life.

MODERN RITUAL FOR THE NEW YEAR

At this time of beginnings, focus on the positive. Think of the good in your life and speak of the good that will come in the future. Thank those who have been kind to you in the past year and list all for which you are grateful. These few minutes for good thoughts and kind words set the tone for the upcoming year and bring you good fortune. Remember the ears of the spirits are open now!

On the first day of the new year, Roman farmers were instructed to make token beginnings of all the kinds of work they expected to perform in the upcoming year, such as planting seeds or pruning vines. So, following in this Roman tradition, on the first day of the year, instead of just listing those New Year's resolutions, make a token beginning of all the things you wish to pursue in the upcoming year. This small ritual not only gets you to focus your plans for the upcoming year, but ensures good luck *(bona fortuna)* in all those new endeavors.

- If you plan to begin an exercise program, take a short walk.
- If you plan to redecorate your home, move some furniture around.
- If you plan to watch your diet, prepare a low-calorie meal or gather recipes.
- Be sure to sweeten your year by giving yourself or someone special a small gift that involves honey. Try caressing your skin with a dollop of creamy honeysuckle lotion.

RITES AND RITUALS OF JANUARY

Thresholds and Beginnings

Doorways and beginnings were highly charged and magical transition points; they were boundaries between two worlds, and very sacred to the ancient Romans. Crossing over the threshold and walking out the front door was leaving the safety of private space and moving into the public world. Departing on a

---

JANUS AND THRESHOLDS

Since doorways marked transitions and beginnings, they were heavily charged with magic and spirits. It was imperative for the Romans to keep the spirit of the doorway appeased and not to offend the great gatekeeper himself. To trip or stumble at the threshold was considered a very bad omen, especially during an important ritual such as marriage. Hence, the groom always carried the bride over the threshold so that she would not trip and offend the spirit of her new home. The bride would also appease the spirit of the doorway, Janus, by anointing the doorposts with wolf's fat, pig's fat, or olive oil (easier to obtain) and by tying pieces of wool to them.

---

journey and passing through the town gate was equivalent to leaving the civilized world and entering the wild and untamed countryside. Likewise, beginning the new year or undertaking a new endeavor meant leaving behind the past and what was familiar and moving toward what was unknown and in the future. Passing through a portal was a critical moment, not to be taken lightly and not a time for frivolity or deception. This was sacred space and sacred time. By crossing through a portal or embarking on a new endeavor, we enter the realm of Janus, God of Portals and God of Beginnings. He is the "Opener of the softly gliding year" (Ovid *Fasti* 1.65).

January 1, KALENDS; *January 5,* NONES

JANUS

AGONALIA

To the ancient Romans, doorways, beginnings, and the month of January were under the spiritual power of Janus, God of Beginnings and Thresholds and namesake of this month.

This first day of the new year was a day of good words, as Ovid tells us: "Now must good words be spoken on a good day. Let ears be rid of law suits and banish mad disputes straightaway! See how the sky sparkles with fragrant fires and how saffron from Cilicia crackles on the kindled hearth"(*Fasti* 1.75LCL). In fact, only good words should be uttered at the start of anything new, because as all Romans knew, omens were abundant at beginnings, "Words have weight, and the ears of the deities are open" at this time.

On the first day of the new year, Janus received offerings of honey sealed in snow-white jars together with dates and figs. The Romans would give similar gifts to friends and family. Honey was the proper offering and gift to secure a propitious beginning and to ensure that the year would be sweet. On this day, it also became traditional to give cash to family and friends. As Ovid tells us over two thousand years ago, "How little you know of the age in which you live if you think that honey is sweeter than cash" (*Fasti* 1.192).

Imagine that the doorway of your home, that area where the door swings open to let you pass through, as very sacred space. At this critical entranceway, most Roman homes had a small shrine built into the wall of the entrance hall. Here, a family member could stop for a moment of prayer, perhaps leaving a cake of libum (a special offering cake to Janus) to honor the point of transition, the division between two worlds, and the God of the Threshold.

Consider for a moment that our front door marks a point of transition and that whenever we cross it, we enter a different world. Even though our steps follow a similar path every morning, one that may seem trite and routine, it is never exactly the same. We do begin something new by crossing that threshold each and every morning. When we leave for work in the morning or hustle the kids off to school, we don't know what will happen, for it is a new day and in a way a new beginning. We move from the security and protection of our house to the public and uncertain world beyond the door. Likewise, after rushing around the workplace, getting the children to their activities, and pushing a cart through the grocery store, we seek the comfort and shelter of our private domestic space— back home. We notice the difference immediately. When we turn the key in the lock, open the door, and go inside, we put down our belongings, hang up our coat, and take a deep breath, we are home at last. It is that space, where we opened the door, crossed the threshold, and entered, just there, those few feet that the Romans considered sacred space.

ANCIENT PRAYER AND OFFERINGS TO JANUS AND BEGINNINGS

The Romans made offerings to Janus at the outset of any new voyage or endeavor. In fact the high priest, the Pontifex Maximus, kept sacred cakes of libum on hand stored in a jar under his bed for emergencies. It was customary to offer Janus a cake of libum on your birthday. Libum was traditionally baked in the shape of clasped hands with entwined fingers.

AN ANCIENT PRAYER TO JANUS

Offer a sacrificial cake to Janus with these words: "Father Janus, in offering to you this sacrificial cake I make good prayers that thou be kind and favorable to me, my children, and my house and household."

Afterward, offer the wine to Janus thus: "Father Janus, as I besought thee with good prayers in offering the sacrificial cake, let me honor thee for the same purpose with sacrificial wine." (Cato De Agricultura 134)

MODERN RITUAL AND OFFERING FOR BEGINNINGS AND BIRTHDAYS

Starting something new can often be intimidating and fretful. To ensure a propitious outcome to any new undertaking, honor the Spirit of Beginnings. Bake these special offering cakes, and pray that all goes well.

We celebrate birthdays with cake, candles, and wishes. Why not extend this custom as the ancient Romans did to beginnings of any kind? Gather together family and friends and announce your new endeavor. Then bask in the good wishes and warmth of a supportive group as you serve these cakes. What a great way to start down a new path!

Cato provides an ancient recipe:

To make libum. Cream well in a mortar, 2 pounds of cheese. Add to the cheese and mix well, I pound of flour. Or if you wish a lighter dough, use $^1/_2$ pound of flour. Add one egg and mix well. Form the cake. Place it on a large leaf and bake slowly in a hot oven. (*De Agricultura* 75)

Here is a modern recipe for sacred cakes:

LIBUM *(serves 6)*

16 ounces cream cheese	pinch of salt
I cup flour	bay leaves
I egg	

Cream the cheese in a bowl until soft. Beat the egg, add it to the cream cheese, and mix well. Slowly add the flour to the egg mixture to form a soft dough. Shape dough into small cakes 2 inches round. Grease a cookie sheet. Place the sacred cakes on top of a well-oiled bay leaf on the cookie sheet. Bake cakes at 350 degrees for 25 to 30 minutes. Serve as an offering with honey. Also good with wine and aperitifs.

MODERN RITUALS TO HONOR THE DOORWAY

Stop and take a few minutes to focus on your threshold—the entrance to your home and a clearly defined boundary between the public and private worlds. The doorway is a place of transition and beginnings and is very sacred space. An entranceway into the home is treated with the utmost respect and care in many cultures. Remember, what you put here are not simply decorations—they are offerings to the God of the Threshold.

- Browse through any handbook on the ancient Chinese practice of feng-shui and pick up tips on the placement of items and decorative treatment of your front door.
- Follow the custom of the ancient Romans and take some care to decorate and bless the doorway into your home. Give some thought to both the exterior and interior sides of the doorway. What message or impression do you wish to create?
- A wreath made of nature's gifts of greenery, dried flowers, and ribbons can be most welcoming.

- Place a special photograph, picture, or meaningful saying on the inside of the front door. It can bring a smile as you prepare to leave for the day.

Sacred Boundaries: The Neighborhood

Are you on friendly terms with your neighbors? In fact, do you even know them? Often, we are so busy with our own lives that we become out of touch with our neighbors and isolated from our community.

The Romans considered neighborhood boundaries as sacred space and celebrated the ancient festival of the Compitalia at the beginning of the new year. The Lares, the same spirits that protected the house and property, also helped ensure good relations between those whose homes bordered each other. Actually, the ritual was a time to get together with neighbors at a big potluck dinner, reaffirm friendships, and discuss future concerns of the community.

January 3–5, III NONES–NONES

SPIRITS OF THE CROSSROADS

COMPITALIA

The Romans viewed crossroads as they did doorways. Both were places of transition and hence full of spirits and magic. They were to be approached cautiously. In the Roman countryside, crossroads were called *compita*—spirit-charged places where boundaries between farms touched each other or where country lanes converged. At these boundary points, small shrines were erected with four altars facing the four directions. At the *compita*, farmers hung up broken plows to honor the spirits and to show the end of the planting season for the winter.

The Compitalia, an ancient agrarian festival for the spirits of the crossroads, was held January 3–5, or the first few days after the Kalends. The farm family's ritual started at nightfall, when each member of the household made and hung up before the household shrine a woolen doll. Heads of garlic were also strung to propitiate the Lares, the household deities, and the spirits of the crossroads.

In towns and cities, the Compitalia became a communal festival in which neighbors whose homes were in the same block got together. A large "potluck" was held to which each family contributed a honey cake.

Looking at Ourselves and Our Relationships

Darkness predominates this month, when the days glide by so quickly and the nights seem to last forever. The solar cycle, which causes long periods of darkness, was at the core of January's ancient rituals, especially those honoring the spirits of the dead and the past, Vediovus and the Di Manes, or Dark Shades. In restructuring our sense of time and coming in sync with the natural cycles, we ourselves must become attuned to the limited periods of light and, more important, the unrelenting dark.

We often associate darkness with negative forces, yet for the seeds in the earth, the dark period is a necessary time of gestation. This is true for us as well! When we enter a period of darkness during January, we must learn to take advantage of this time and to lay the groundwork and prepare for the upcoming year. This month, we must summon the courage to look deep inside ourselves and journey underground into those very dark places, to our very roots. This is why Vediovus and the Di Manes were honored in the beginning of January. This is why two-faced Janus can look backward and forward at once.

January is the time to deal directly with what is over, finished, and dead—whether ideas, relationships, or dear ones—all that was once part of us. We must internalize the good and hold close the cherished memories, yet not allow ourselves to be numbed by past events.

Yes, we must be grateful for the good in our daily lives. But ancient people knew only too well, the Dark Forces, the Di Manes, are equally potent and affect us in powerful ways. Facing them directly is the best way to weaken their power, for to ignore the dark side only hampers our true growth. We must acknowledge the presence of the dark spirits, draw from their power, and appease them before we move on.

ANCIENT RITUAL: LIBATION

A libation poured on the ground, and thus drunk by the earth, was an offering reserved for the dead and those spirits who dwelled underground. The Romans most often cremated their dead and buried the ashes in family tombs just outside the town walls. In fact, the roads leading into any Roman town were lined on either side up to the entrance gate with tombs of deceased citizens. Often, a permanent libation hole was dug into the ground to serve as a gateway to the dead spirits. The family would then make libation throughout the year to deceased relatives.

Odysseus (Ody. 11.26–34) conjured up the dead when he poured a libation, first of honey, then of wine, and finally of water. He then sprinkled barley over the libation as he intoned the dead spirits. Possibly the most beautiful ritual of libation, performed in a sacred grove of trees, is detailed by Sophocles in *Oedipus at Colonus* (466–92). First, water is drawn from a freshly flowing spring, and cauldrons standing in the sanctuary are filled with water and honey and covered with wool. Holding olive branches in one hand, the libation maker then turns toward the east and tips the vessel with the water toward the west. Then olive branches are scattered where the earth received its sacred drink. The worshiper makes a silent prayer and quietly departs, not looking back.

How many relationships languished because we were too afraid to express our needs? How many times were we filled with creativity and had wonderful ideas, yet never saw them to fruition? The Di Manes were tugging at our ankles. Each of us carries a dark side within where our very own personal Di Manes reside. This is that part of us that works against progress, that holds us back, and that we avoid. Instinctively we know that to move forward and for our spirit to survive, we must face those very personal dark spirits lurking inside.

January 1, KALENDS

VEDIOVUS

The pull of the past and the shades of the dead that seemed so close to the Romans throughout this wintry barren month were represented by Vediovus, a spirit of the dead and a god from times forgotten. Vediovus was a god of the dead or, as the Romans called them, the Di Manes. He appeared as a young man carrying arrows and attended by a goat.

MODERN RITUAL TO APPEASE THE DARK SPIRITS AND INSTILL GOODWILL

Eat something sweet to banish the darkness and share it with friends to bring about harmonious relations. When Marney served her warm honey cake with fragrant spiced tea to our women's group at one chilly January meeting, we each savored the sweetness that month. A piece of baklava, sticky and gooey with honey and nuts, from your favorite bakery is a time-honored treat to honor the deities of January and yourself.

MARNEY'S HONEY CAKE

4 eggs, beaten
1 1/4 cups granulated sugar
1/2 cup safflower oil
1 cup raw honey
2 1/2 cups flour
2 1/2 teaspoons baking powder

1/2 teaspoon baking soda
1 teaspoon allspice
3/4 teaspoon ground cinnamon
1 teaspoon ground ginger
1/8 teaspoon ground nutmeg

Preheat oven to 350 degrees. Grease and flour a 9 x 13 inch baking pan. Combine all ingredients well; pour into pan and bake for 40 minutes. Traditionally served unfrosted.

ANCIENT HEALING RITUAL: INCUBATION

The healing ritual known as incubation followed a very specific format. First, the patient spent three days undergoing purification and
abstaining from sex, goat meat, and cheese. Then, with a wreath of
laurel encircling her head, the patient offered cakes and garlands
entwined with olive twigs to the healing deities. On the day of the
healing ceremony the patient offered two cakes, on an altar in the
open air, to Good Fortune, Memory, Success, and Recollection. A
third cake was taken into the sanctuary and offered to the Goddess of
Right Order. The patient, still wearing the laurel wreath, lay down on
a pallet spread before the large cult statue of Aesculapius and fell
asleep. This individual encounter with the deity was surely most personal and profound. The cure so eagerly sought was revealed in the
dream, which the patient would interpret.

Dream and Heal

Slowing down, wrapping ourselves in a warm protective blanket, and
snuggling in for a good sleep is just what nature ordered for the month of
January. We can use this time to sleep, dream, and heal ourselves both
physically and emotionally.

Healing was a religious experience for the ancient Romans involving
prayer, sacrifice, and belief, beginning with an individual's personal
encounter through dream with the healing deities. It is fitting that we
focus on our health at the onset of the new year, especially after facing
the fearsome and sorrowful Di Manes. This month we need to learn to
take care of ourselves.

January 1, KALENDS

AESCULAPIUS AND SALUS

The healing deities Aesculapius, his mother, Coronis, and his daughter, Salus (Hygeia), were honored during the first weeks of January. The god Aesculapius, always accompanied by a sacred snake coiled around his staff, was worshiped at large Greek cult centers and healing shrines at Epidaurus and Cos. In 291 B.C.E., the god was officially brought to Rome in the following manner:

> The Romans on account of a pestilence, at the instructions of the Sibylline books, sent ten envoys under the leadership of Quintus Ogulnius to bring Aesculapius from Epidaurus. When they had arrived there and were marveling at the huge statue of the god, a serpent glided from the temple, an object of veneration rather than horror, and to the astonishment of all made its way through the midst of the city to the Roman ship, and curled itself up in the tent of Ogulnius. . . . And when the ship was sailing up the Tiber, the serpent leaped on the nearby island, where a temple was established to him. The pestilence subsided with astonishing speed. (Anon. *On Famous Men* 12.1–3 L&R)

The island in the Tiber selected by the serpent remains a place of healing today as the site of the Hospital of St. Bartolomeo. Ancient columns can be found in the adjacent church. If one looks closely at the carving on the wall at the southwestern tip of the island, the sacred snake is still visible.

MODERN HEALING RITUAL: INCUBATION AND DREAMWORK

Incubation is the term used for the ancient practice of sleeping on the temple floor, often together with the sacred snake and dogs. I often wonder how the patients ever fell asleep, not to mention what forms their dream imagery took. Yet dream imagery is an important source of healing.

Start with a positive attitude and don't be discouraged if you can't recall your dreams. Tell yourself during the day that you will remember your dreams, and upon awakening lie still for a while, focusing your conscious mind on whatever ideas or emotions have emerged from your sleep and allowing them through association to prompt dream recall. Keep a dream diary in which you either write or draw your dreams.

The ancient healing shrines were not unlike our modern spas, except that first and foremost they were religious centers, sites of holistic healing and mind/body work under the power of the god and goddess where all aspects of the patient were treated. We can recapture the sage advice offered by Aesculapius and Salus. Ancient healing shrines were usually located in quiet valleys or sites away from a large city. Patients seeking cures from a variety of ailments from baldness to lameness and disease often stayed for months. The shrines were staffed with priests, priestesses, and attendants to guide patients through the cure. Diet was supervised and exercise such as walking, games, and sports was encouraged. As mental stimulation was considered important for a well-balanced life, the shrines contained libraries where philosophers and educators lectured. Since drama, poetry, and music had a healing and cathartic effect upon patients, the larger shrines had theaters for performances.

January 11, III Ides

J U T U R N A

Juturna, a water nymph and healer, the Spirit of Living Water, was also addressed as Frigida or Serena. There were several shrines in ancient Rome to Juturna. One no longer in existence stood near the modern Piazza di S. Ignazio, and perhaps the Church of S. Maria in Aquiro, a little to the north in the Piazza Caprinica, preserves the memory of this water goddess. The water that fed Juturna's shrine in antiquity was carried by the Aqua Virgo ("Virgin Water"), an aqueduct built in 19 B.C.E., which still brings water to Rome and fills the fountain of Trevi.

The Lacus Juturnus, a famous spring in the Roman times, has been restored today. It lies to the southeast of the Forum near the Building of the Vestals and can be visited. The sacred precinct of Juturna consists of the spring and basin, a temple façade that held the statue of the goddess, and several other rooms that served in antiquity as headquarters for the Roman water service.

MODERN HEALING RITUAL WITH WATER

Give yourself some fallow time, indulge in moments of meditation, a quiet evening with a book before the fire, a bubble bath by candlelight. In fact, immersion in water, the primordial source of life, was a traditional way to begin healing. The goddess Juturna was both a water nymph and healer—a connection you will come to understand once you luxuriate in a hot sudsy bath after a hectic day.

Make your bath a special sacred time when you cleanse not just your body, but your mind and soul as well. Flowers, perfumes, bath oils, incense, candles, music, and prayer were all parts of a ritual bath. Juturna teaches us that slowing down, focusing on ourselves, indulging our senses, and creating a sacred ritual from a seemingly mundane act such as bathing can be quite healing indeed! With the warm bath water flowing around you, let yourself be lulled into a quiet time. Envision the seeds deep in the cold earth as they lie dormant, the mother bear as she curls in endless sleep in her cave, and you know deep down somewhere that this is the right thing to do.

As you take this first step in becoming attuned to the natural world, you intuitively know that a quieting, inward-turning time is essential for well-being and growth. When you give yourself this gift, you too are rejoining the cycle of nature. January was meant to be this way.

Glimpse the Future

By mid-month we notice the subtle change in daylight. Even though darkness still reigns, the sun rises earlier now and gives us a few more precious moments of light in the evening. We begin to catch a flicker of light in the midst of darkness, a glimpse of the future year.

FORETELLING THE FUTURE: THE AUSPICES

This is what distinguishes us from the Etruscans, masters in observation of lightning. We think that lightning arises because clouds bump against each other; they on the other hand hold the belief that the clouds bump only in order that lightning may be caused. For as they connect everything with the spirits, they have the notion that lightning is not significant on account of its appearance as such, but only appears at all because it has to give divine signs. (Seneca *Naturales Quaestiones* 2.32 Campbell)

Divine signs from nature—thunder, lightning, the flight of birds, the song of birds, sounds or actions of other animals—were quite auspicious. A sign such as a flash of lightning may occur suddenly and unexpectedly to an individual. Or a sign such as the flight of birds may be sought on purpose and with a specific question in mind. The natural sign was then interpreted by the individual, who could also consult with a priest, augur, or even literature. Taking the auspices was also done publicly by magistrates before acts of state. Sacred chickens were even kept by the Roman state and their behavior while feeding often gave the go-ahead or warning sign for official government functions. Prophecy and divination through nature were taken very seriously by the Romans.

Carmenta, the Happy Prophetess, whose name comes from the word *carmen,* a divine incantation, prophecy, or song, was an enchantress who listened to her inner voice. She was honored especially by women, and could see the future in positive terms.

Prophetesses were wild women possessed by the spirits, women who gave voice to their intuitive sides. They were respected and trusted in ancient times. We should likewise come to trust our instinct and intuition and not ignore those voices inside whispering their deep-felt messages.

Carmenta was also the Goddess of Childbirth. It was she who protected the unborn babe in the womb, and she, together with her sisters, Antevorta and Postverta, made sure of an easy birth. These goddesses were the ones to determine the position of the stars at birth and thereby define the destiny of the child.

January 11, 15; III Ides, XVI Kalends February

CARMENTA

CARMENTALIA

Carmenta, the Happy Prophetess, was Moon Goddess, Goddess of Beginnings, and Goddess of Childbirth. Carmenta, who could foresee the future, chanted words of encouragement with an inspired voice in prophetic strains. "Every land is to the brave his country, as to the fish the sea, as to the bird whatever place stands open in the void world. Nor does the tempest rage the whole year long; trust me, there will be springtime yet" (Ovid *Fasti* 1.495).

There could be no sign of death inside her temple, where leather sandals and animal skins were forbidden. In fact, the Romans thought that pregnant women should never wear the skins of dead animals or their children would be born dead. "It is not lawful to bring leather into her shrine, lest her pure hearths should be defiled by skins of slaughtered beasts. If you have any love of ancient rites, attend the prayers offered to her: you shall hear names you never knew before" (Ovid *Fasti* 1.630 LCL).

Carmenta was attended by her two sisters, Antevorta and Postverta, "Forward Facing" and "Backward Facing," referring to their powers over the position of the child in the womb. Other female spirits who were present at childbirth included Lucina, "She who opened the baby's eyes to the first light"; Levana, "She who aided the father in picking up the baby"; and Candelifera, "She who watched over the nursery lamp."

January 24–26, MOVEABLE RITUAL AFTER THE IDES

CERES AND TELLUS

SEMENTIVAE AND PAGANALIA

The Sementivae and Paganalia were held on these last days of the first lunation of January. These were farmer's rites for the sowing of seed, prosperity, and peace. In the Roman countryside, sacrifice was made to Tellus, or Mother Earth, and to Ceres on two separate days within the last week of January.

> Let the community keep festival, purify the community farmers and offer cakes on community hearths. Propitiate Earth and Ceres, the mothers of grain, with cakes of their own grain. Ceres and Earth perform a common function: one lends the grain its vital life force, the other lends it room to grow. Partners in work . . . (Ovid *Fasti* 1.675)

Pray for Peace and Prosperity

The end of January has come, and it is time to ground ourselves in the earth, look forward to the upcoming year, and pray to Mother Earth and Ceres for peace and prosperity. We come to the altar of peace on January 30 with this song:

> *Come peace, your flowing tresses wreathed with laurel. Let your gentle presence triumph in the whole world. Let there be no foes. Add incense to the flames that burn on the altar of peace, pour a wine libation, pray to the deities, may peace last forever.* (Ovid Fasti 1.720)

FEBRUARY

THE MONTH TO PURIFY

In sum, anything used to purify our bodies was named
februa by our ancestors.
The month is named after this . . . (Ovid Fasti 2.29–30)

Rural Menologia
SUN IN AQUARIUS
28 DAYS
NONES: FEBRUARY 5
DAYLIGHT: 10 3/4 HOURS
DARKNESS: 13 1/4 HOURS

During February, ancient Roman farmers were busy cleaning up the debris from their meadows and fields left behind by winter storms. The vines above ground were tended, as were the olive and fruit trees; the willow was pruned and some early grain was sown. (Menologia)

❧❧❧❧❧

February is a pivotal month, a transitional phase between the seasons, a gray shrouded time balanced between winter's deepest sleep and spring's reawakening. This is the month for preparation. The frivolity of winter solstice celebrations has long since past. For the Romans, the daily and mundane acts of sweeping, dusting, and scrubbing the house clean were elevated into magical purification rituals that dominated the entire second month. While waiting for spring and rebirth, it is vital to purify all surroundings and to ritually sweep away the decay, the bad, the guilt, or the pain. This is a very sacred time!

For the ancient Romans, it was essential to be in good favor with nature's powerful forces. During February, those powers that oversee positive growth and fertility must be placated and welcomed and hostile deadly forces must be banished and kept away from one's body, home, land, and community. Bad spirits and decay were swept away from houses, farmlands, and towns. A solemn and very serious mood prevailed during the entire month of February. In the sacred calendar, this was the month to set things right within home, community, and especially family.

The Romans valued a strong supportive family including immediate relatives as well as the extended family, all related by blood or marriage. In fact, individual success in the political, social, and economic worlds depended on a tightly knit family. It was vital to seek the goodwill and kindly intentions of family members to ensure prosperity and success for the upcoming year. For the Romans, this meant establishing a bond with the dead and the living kin. This was done ritually every February with a specific period set aside for reunion and a healing of old wounds between family members living or dead. February was a special month to remember loving kin, to set aside sacred time to honor those who had died, especially parents or grandparents. This was the month to set things right.

Here is a powerful tale that embodies the vitality and endurance of family bonds. It is the story of the nymph Callisto, her dire and wrongful suffering, the intensity of her parental love, and the setting things right by her ultimate redemption through a final and perpetual reunion with her son.

Callisto

Callisto was a young woodland nymph and dear companion of Diana, Goddess of the Wild Woods. Upon joining Diana's sacred band of nymphs, Callisto placed one hand on the goddess's bow and took a solemn oath, "I swear by this bow to remain a virgin." Diana commanded her and said, "Keep the promise that you've made and you will be my favorite companion."

Callisto could have kept her promise if she had not been so pretty. She avoided all men, but the lustful god Jupiter saw her. His passion was aroused for the beautiful and wild woodland nymph. He raped her, and she became pregnant with the child of Jupiter. But she was ashamed and hid her pregnancy.

One warm day, Diana was returning from the hunt around noontime, when the sun was at its zenith. Walking to her secret place in the mountains, a deep dark grove of oak trees fed by a natural spring of icy water, the goddess shouted, "Virgin nymphs, let's bathe here in the woods."

Feeling shame, Callisto blushed at the word "virgin." All the other nymphs quickly undressed and splashed into the cool water. Callisto delayed and hesitated. When her tunic was off, her swollen belly gave her away, visible evidence of her pregnant condition. Diana was angered and spoke harshly to her, "Callisto, you liar, leave this band of virgins immediately. Do not foul our chaste waters with your presence."

Ten times the moon went from new to full, and the supposed virgin became the mother of a baby boy. When Jupiter's wife, Juno, saw the child, she was driven crazy. Hurt that her husband had been unfaithful and driven by jealous rage, Juno transformed Callisto into a bear. Why? Callisto was innocent; Jupiter had raped her, taken her against her will. When Juno looked upon Callisto's beastlike face, she taunted her husband, "Now, you can go to bed with that beast."

Callisto wandered alone and friendless through the mountain wilderness—now a shaggy bear. Her son, never seeing his mother, was taken from her and raised by others. When her dear son reached fifteen years, Callisto encountered him again—a chance meeting! He had set off early one morning to hunt wild beasts in those very same mountains.

She knew him at once, though she was a bear and he a strong young man. Out of her wits and desperate, Callisto stood and looked into his eyes. She growled, for that was the only sound she could make. The growl was a mother's voice! The boy was frightened and raised his spear to kill her. How was he to recognize his own mother? He would have unwittingly killed his own dear mother, but at that instant both were whisked to a home in the sky. They shine as neighboring constellations. The Bear leads the way, the Bear Keeper appears to trail after.

What happened to Callisto was unjust. Both god and goddess abandoned her, leaving the helpless nymph to wander the wild mountains alone for fifteen years, bereft of her son and without support of family or friends. But Callisto survived! The love for her son likewise endures through the years of separation and hardship. As the myth closes, both nymph and son are reunited for eternity, transformed into stars that comprise the Bear constellation. Callisto is forever the Mother Bear watching over her child. She is the Mother Goddess made manifest.

This deeply moving tale reminds us about the sacredness and the power that binds a family with ties that on some level can never be lost or denied. Like Callisto, we often struggle against circumstances beyond our control that threaten our friendships and especially our family relationships. We can look to Callisto's years of wandering as our own uncertain journey to preserve the goodness and sanctity found only in deep bonds of love. As we seek resolution and reconciliation, we must come to grips with hurtful or jarring memories. In February, we are compelled to purify ourselves as we come to terms with the grief, anger, or guilt and to move on, feeling ultimate satisfaction in setting family matters right.

RITES AND RITUALS OF FEBRUARY

Purify and Renew

"Will winter never end?" we ask ourselves quietly on those cold gray overcast days, when we awake in the dark and just lie there under the warm safe covers dreading to set foot on the cold floor. It is dark when we leave home in the morning and dark when we return. How easy it is this time of year to lose touch with the natural cycle— not a surprise since we spend most of our time indoors and under artificial light. Depression can creep in ever so lightly, and sometimes we feel powerless to make the changes that seem overdue. February tempts us to give up on New Year's resolutions. Those dark harmful spirits lurking in the shadow of the threshold are taking over! You can regain spiritual power over them by focusing on the rituals of purification, the rituals of February.

We each bear a burden of misgivings, mistakes, painful memories, and ill-spoken words or deeds. We alone know those areas, those dark secrets that make us feel "dirty" and in need of a good cleaning. Feelings of impurity can reach inside us and pull us down into the muck. February is the time to sweep away those bad habits and banish any self-destructive behavior. When we take steps to purge the "bad spirits" and purify ourselves and our immediate surroundings, we set things aright. Purification rituals can be very cleansing; they can be healing rites that touch our most deeply felt emotions and memories.

Purification and renewal is especially important for women. We bear the children, support the family,

---

ANCESTORS

In Roman times, the family ancestors were honored within each household, where lifelike images of the deceased were kept in special rooms off the atrium. A knowledge of family history and family roots was of prime importance. The "genius," or male spirit of the family that was reflected in the men, and the "juno," the female spirit in women, were cherished and honored on special occasions before the family altar.

Just as the seeds tenaciously extend their roots deep within the earth to take hold in February, likewise we can strengthen our own bonds and reach out to learn more about our ancestral roots. We can learn more about our ancestors and research family roots by creating a family tree.

tend the home, and keep the hearth fires burning—and we desperately need positive nurturing energy. The people of antiquity understood the sacred and symbiotic relationship between female energy, survival of the family, and prosperity of the household. February 1 was the day that young girls entered the sacred grove of Juno Sospita, the Goddess of Protection and Fertility, and fed her sacred snake in honor of the truly feminine powers of fertility and regeneration.

The snake—a primal creature mysteriously crawling out of holes issuing from deep within the earth, appearing suddenly, moving silently and quickly, and vanishing just as quickly down into the moist earth again—serves as a talisman and promise of rebirth. With the seasons, the snake sloughs off its old skin to grow a new one. It hibernates—it goes away and comes again as though reborn. The snake was sacred throughout the Neolithic period as an epiphany of the Great Goddess. The snake is positive female energy incarnate!

February 1, KALENDS

JUNO SOSPITA

Juno Sospita Mater Regina was honored on this day. Juno Sospita, the Goddess of Protection and Fertility, was often seen in military garb made out of goatskin, with the goat head and horns pulled up as a helmet. Carrying a spear and shield, she wears shoes with upturned toes and is accompanied by a snake, crow, or raven.

The ritual to Juno Sospita is for protection, fertility, and prosperity, especially for women. Her worship originated in the town of Lanuvium, where an unusual and quite ancient ritual took place to Juno Sospita on February 1. Young girls, preferably virgins, from the town were blindfolded and led by the hand into Juno's sacred grove. They carried with them gifts of barley cakes to feed the sacred snake that lived in the grove. If the cakes were accepted by the snake, in the upcoming year the women would bear healthy children, the crops would be plentiful, and all would be prosperous.

MODERN RITUAL OF RENEWAL

You may choose to interpret the snake-feeding ritual of February 1 on a symbolic, rather than literal level. Think of sloughing off the old and feeling regenerated by the new. Just as the snake sheds its skin, shed those thoughts and objects you wish to discard and be rid of. Kindle the precious sparks of something new and let them warm you on this cold day in early February.

You can also warm yourself with a steaming cup of coffee or tea and a piece of delicious home-baked bread. The regenerative image of the snake is retained in the form of a spiral honey bread.

HONEY SPIRAL BREAD

1 package active dry yeast
$1/2$ cup milk, scalded
$1/4$ cup sugar
$1/2$ teaspoon salt
2 tablespoons butter
3 cups all-purpose flour
1 egg

HONEY TOPPING:
$1/4$ cup butter
$2/3$ cup confectioners' powdered sugar
1 egg white
2 tablespoons warm honey

Soften the yeast in $1/4$ cup of warm water. Pour the scalded milk over the sugar, salt, and butter in a bowl. Let the mixture cool to lukewarm. Add the yeast and two cups of flour, and beat vigorously with an electric mixer. Beat in the egg and enough flour to form a soft dough. Immediately knead dough for 5 to 10 minutes on a lightly floured surface until dough is smooth and elastic and does not stick to an unfloured surface. Turn the dough into a lightly greased bowl that is large enough to accommodate twice the size of the dough. Cover the dough and let it rise for about two hours. After the dough has risen, shape it into a long roll about four or five feet long. Coil the dough into a ten-inch round pan, beginning at the outside edge and covering the bottom of the pan. Cream together the honey topping ingredients. Brush the spiral with topping and let it rise until doubled for about 45 minutes. Bake at 375 degrees for 35 to 45 minutes.

This sweet, sticky treat is best served with lemon-water finger bowls and napkins.

To the Greeks and Romans, the snake assured continuity of life and was viewed in a very positive light—it was a lucky talisman. Small clay replicas of coiled snakes have been found in the ancient *lararia* at Pompeii as well as painted on interior household walls. In fact, the presence of a snake image defined sacred space.

The snake's regenerative energy protected the family, assuring fertility and continuity from generation to generation. This is why snakes were considered a sacred symbol within the family, and why they were honored and fed on February 1.

February 1, KALENDS

HELERNUS

On this day in ancient Rome, worshipers thronged the sacred grove of Helernus, God of Vegetables, at the mouth of the Tiber River. There, priests would offer sacrifices to this most ancient Protector of Vegetables. For the ancient Romans, this was a time to come outdoors after a dark winter, to pray for a good vegetable crop, and, if the weather permitted, to picnic along the Tiber.

February 13, IDES

FAUNUS

On the Ides, the altars of wild Faunus smoke. (Ovid *Fasti* 2.194–95)

Faunus was God of the Wild and Spirit of the Untamed Woodland. His name is derived from *favere* and means the "Kindly One." He was a companion to the shepherd and is depicted as half man and half goat with horns and hooves. As a hunter and agricultural deity, he was honored chiefly in the countryside; his cult never caught on in the towns and cities.

Faunus was an oracular god associated with all the strange noises of the untamed night forest. Those seeking the oracle would enter the grove sacred to Faunus, pose a question, and listen to the night noises. The interpretation was left to the seeker.

Purify and Honor the House

Although spring cleaning has long been a secular ritual in many households, a ritual cleansing of the home is conducted as a preparatory act before a sacred event.

February 5, NONES

FEBRUUS

FEBRUALIA

Honoring the god Februus consisted of a ritual cleansing and purification of the house. *Februa*, or instruments of purification, for example, boughs taken from a pine tree (a "pure tree"), were used to ritually sweep the house clean of bad spirits. Performing this ritual purified the house for the upcoming year.

From olden times, on the Nones of February, the high priest proclaimed the Februalia, a *dies februatus*, or "purification day." On this day, the house was ritually cleaned of all evil spirits, while anything lurking in the atrium that could bring harm was officially banished. Only the good spirits and positive energy must enter the house.

The process of purification was overseen by a priest or member of the family serving as Sweeper-Out. The entire house was cleaned, and a mixture of salt and grain was sprinkled around and then ritually swept out. The house was then considered cleansed.

The ancient Romans held a sacred ritual of cleaning house every February. The Februalia was a festival to cleanse the house and get rid of any bad spirits that might lurk behind the furniture. A priest or family member would officiate at the rite by sprinkling a mixture of salt and grain on the floor and ritually sweeping it out the door. The home was then purified and the evil spirits swept out.

This act of cleaning house both on a practical and symbolic level can be very healing. We do feel better when ridding ourselves of what is dirty and dysfunctional; besides, a thorough scrubbing and a ritual sweep of a pine bough leave a wonderful fresh scent in the air.

MODERN RITUAL TO PURIFY YOUR HOUSE

February is the month to roll up your sleeves and get down to work—housekeeping, that is. It is time for spring cleaning—an annual ritual of throwing out the unwanted junk that has collected over the winter, giving away the outgrown clothes, and scouring the filmy windows to let in the ever increasing sunlight. When you have finished housecleaning, be sure to perform a ritual cleansing. Walk through your home with any *februa*, or instruments of purification, of your choosing, a pine bough, a piece of white wool, or a feather. Sweep those bad spirits right out the door and welcome in positive healing energy. Say a little prayer to your very own household deities.

HONOR THE OVEN GODDESS

I, too, am nervous during winter; when the gray morning mist creates a mutable barrier between dreaming and waking, I get up slightly disoriented, on edge. It is then I need a staunch pie. Calming pie. (Molly O'Neill, Food Editor, New York Times, *January 24, 1999)*

February 5–17, Moveable Ritual from Nones–XIII Kalends March

FORNAX

FORNACALIA

So they honored the oven as Fornax, a goddess; overjoyed with the goddess Fornax, the farmers prayed that she would prepare the grain. (Ovid *Fasti* 2.520–26).

Feriae Conceptivae are moveable rituals that can occur within a time frame. In early February, between the 5th and the 17th, families and friends would gather for a communal feast to celebrate the Fornacalia, or Feast of the Ovens, in honor of Fornax, Goddess of the Ovens.

These meals were "simple, economical and lacking all vulgar display," according to one Roman author. "Meals set before the gods on ancient wooden tables, in baskets and on small earthen plates consisted of barley-bread, cakes and grains with some first-fruits." The libation (wine offering) was mixed in little earthen cups and jugs, not in ones of silver or gold.

After the cleansing and purification of the home, the Romans turned their attention to the oven—the source of sustenance for the family. The Fornacalia, or Feast of the Ovens, was held during the first two weeks of February in honor of Fornax, the Goddess of the Ovens.

In earliest times, each family brought an unbaked loaf to the common oven that served the baking needs of the small community. Later, as the demand for bread grew with the burgeoning population, privately owned bakeries supplied bread and pastries to the town dwellers. Even so, Fornax was still honored on these days in Rome with an offering of bread and a communal feast. The goddess Fornax had power over the oven. It was she who made sure a fire would not spread and destroy the home, she who stopped the bread from burning, and she who saw that all the baked goods came out perfect. Say a prayer to this goddess!

MODERN RITUAL TO THE OVEN GODDESS

A feast is definitely in order after cleaning the house. Bake something. Few things can equal the satisfaction of a clean house filled with the wonderful smells of something special baking in the oven, perhaps an apple pie—comfort food. Just what we need in February. Or have a dinner party and invite friends and family to contribute a loaf to be baked in your oven. What a good way to inject warmth into your home and honor all your hard work. This communal ritual is both warm and comforting. It is a rite to nourish your soul as well as your body.

APPLE CAKE, MOIST, CHEWY, AND DELICIOUS

3 cups all-purpose flour

1 teaspoon salt

1 teaspoon baking soda

1 teaspoon baking powder

1 teaspoon cinnamon

1 1/2 cups granulated sugar

1/2 cup dark brown sugar

1 1/4 cup canola oil

3 large eggs

2 teaspoons vanilla

3 cups apples, peeled, cored, and diced

3/4 cup coarsely chopped walnuts

Sift flour, baking soda, baking powder, salt, and cinnamon. In a separate bowl, blend sugar with canola oil. Add eggs to the sugar-and-oil mixture, and beat well after each egg. Slowly add the flour. Mixture will be thick. With a large wooden spoon, stir in apples and walnuts. Mix well. Pour into greased and floured pan, and bake at 300 degrees for 1 hour and 20 to 40 minutes.

Setting Relationships Right

February is a truly solemn time, when relations with the living and the dead must be made right. Having the good wishes of close relatives, even those who were dead, was an essential preparatory act for the Romans. It was a period of remembrance, with official days set aside to honor the spirits of the dead. It is, however, not a fearful time, for it was the "friendly dead" who were honored, especially beloved parents.

February 13–21, IDES–VIII KALENDS MARCH

PARENTALIA

The Parentalia was a festival to appease the dead held in mid-February. The period for appeasement began at the sixth hour (perhaps dawn) of February 13 and lasted until February 21 (when the Feralia, a closely related festival, began). On the first day of this week of remembrance, a Vestal Virgin performed a ceremony by pouring a libation to honor the dead. During this period, all temples were closed, no offering fires were lit on altars, and marriages were banned. The Parentalia was a privately held rite (the Feralia was a public ritual to the dead).

Mourners would pay homage to the deceased at the family tomb always located outside the city walls, where they offered personal prayers and performed private sacred rites. Family members left simple offerings.

> The tomb is honored. Placate the souls of your ancestors and bear small gifts to the tombs. The Dark Shades seek little, they prefer devotion over a costly gift, the spirits who live below are not greedy. A tile wreathed with garlands, a sprinkling of grain, a few grains of salt, bread soaked in wine, and some loose violets, these are offerings enough, set these on a piece of pottery and leave it near the grave. I do not discourage larger gifts, but the Dark Shades are appeased with just these. Say the right prayers and appropriate words over the hearth constructed for this purpose. (Ovid *Fasti* 2.537)

This was also called the "violet festival," when the grave was covered with violets. The "rose festival" to the dead occurred later in the year.

MODERN RITUAL TO HONOR DEAR DEAD ONES

We too can view February as a time for reunion, a time of healing of old wounds and cleansing. Now you can make amends with family members, including those who died before you had the chance to set things aright. In the Roman world, you are given another chance to establish good feelings with deceased parents or relatives. You should approach deceased parents, friends, and relatives with honor and respect.

The Roman family would journey to the tomb and make a libation, taking small offerings and gifts. You may wish to remember your beloved. Now is a good time to gather with your family and friends to share past moments of pain and sorrow. Let the good memories flood your mind and caress you. You might cry a little and feel quite sad. Allow this to happen. You may sense pain in your body and your soul—let it come, for now is the right time to deal with the dead and earlier times in your life. Just as all nature shudders in the cold and dark quietly awaiting the period of rebirth, so should we.

MODERN RITUAL TO HONOR DEAR LIVING KIN

Families often gather together around a meal, such as at Thanksgiving, and at the religious holidays of Christmas, Passover, or Easter. Yet the idea of coming together for the sole purpose of resolving family problems is unique and perhaps should be revived. Each person brings not only a potluck dish, but family problems and concerns to share. A prayer for family harmony sets the tone, and wine and good food pave the way to resolve conflicts that often arise from lack of communication. In place of a family gathering, you may convey kind thoughts and wishes for family members through a letter, card, telephone call, or prayer.

February 21, IX KALENDS MARCH

FERALIA

The period for the Parentalia ended and the Feralia began on February 21. "The Feralia is so named from the dark powers, the *inferi,* and from the verb 'to carry,' as offerings were carried to the tomb on this day" (Varro *De Lingua Latina* 6.13). Its purpose was to appease dark forces and negative energy that could be stirred up by evil thoughts and words.

An unusual ritual to Tacita Muta, the Silent Goddess, is linked with the Parentalia and Feralia. In accordance with this rite, a wise old woman conducts the rite to "bind fast hostile tongues and unfriendly mouths":

An old woman, leading a group of young girls, performs this ritual in honor of Tacita, the Goddess of Silence; although she herself is not silent.

First, the old woman places three pieces of incense at the threshold of the room, just where the little mouse has made herself a secret entrance-way. Then, the older woman binds up a piece of dark lead with enchanted threads. She places seven black beans in her mouth. She then lights a fire and roasts in a pan the head of a small fish whose mouth she has sewed up with thread and pierced through and through with a bronze needle.

The old woman pours out drops of wine onto the fish head. Any wine that is left over, she shares with her younger companions; yet she always gets the larger share. As she completes the Silencing Ritual, she says, "We have bound tight hostile tongues and unfriendly mouths." So exits the old woman drunk. (Ovid *Fasti* 2.571–84)

A silencing ritual may be appropriate. Haven't we each at some time spoken hurtful words to our parents? How we regret those words, especially if our mother or father died before a reconciliation was made. How we crave a second chance and an opportunity to make things right. In seeking the blessings of our parents, deceased or living, a commitment to avoid harsh words and harmful speech can serve a beneficial purpose. These important rituals provide that chance to remedy prior pain and hurt among family members.

MODERN RITUAL FOR BANISHING HARMFUL WORDS AND THOUGHTS

Although the ancient silencing ritual of the crone does seem foreign and strange, a banishing ritual involving wine is not uncommon. During the Jewish Passover service, drops of wine are used to symbolize the ten harmful plagues.

You, likewise, might pour out drops of wine while naming those things that plague you—the thoughts, memories, emotions, deeds, words, or even people you wish to banish from your life. Jotting them down on paper that you then bind up with thread and burn in a fire is also a banishment ritual. Watching the harmful words go up in flames provides a great release. Save some wine to drink yourself and celebrate the banishment of harmful spirits.

HEALING FAMILY FEUDS

Sweet it is, no doubt, to recall our thoughts to the living soon as they have dwelt upon the grave and on the dear ones dead and gone; sweet, too, after so many lost to look upon those of our blood who are left and to count kin with them. (Ovid Fasti 2.620 LCL)

February 22, VIII KALENDS MARCH

CARISTIA

The Caristia, also called the Cara Cognatio, or the Festival to Dear Kindred or Loving Family (Caring Kin), took place the day after the Feralia and was of a very different nature—it was a ritual for setting things aright with the living. "Our ancestors established a ceremonial feast and called it the Caristia, to which nobody but relatives and in-laws is invited, so that, if any quarrel had arisen among the kinsfolk, it might be resolved at the sacred rites of the meal, and harmony was established among those in the company fostering harmony" (Valerius Maximus 2.1.8).

All family members offered prayer and sacrifice to the household deities. A family meal was held and everybody brought something to the "Love Feast." The family gathered to honor the household deities and to offer them grapes, grain, honeycombs, cakes, wine, incense, and flowers.

Once good relations were ensured with dead relatives, then it was time to heal wounds and end quarrels among living relations. The Caristia, the Feast of Caring Kin, followed closely on the Parentalia and Feralia. A day was set aside officially for mending of family quarrels and misunderstandings when blessings of the living were sought and family grievances ironed out. This very special family reunion with a few sacred minutes of prayer and ritual was held on February 22.

Concord and harmony among kin was considered vital to the Romans. Perhaps today we lose touch with our family—it is so easy to drift apart, especially when great distances can separate us. All families share problems and quarrels do arise among family members. The ancient Romans set aside one day a year to formally deal with family problems, at a reunion centered around a sacred meal, the *sacra mensa*, where the family problems were resolved. February 22 is the perfect day to set things straight as the year gets under way.

PURIFY AND MAKE FERTILE

The ability to bear children and produce a family is a strong desire for many men and women—not all. In the oldest times, children were essential for the very survival of the family as they worked alongside their parents performing many functions on the farm and helping to supply food for the family. It was also crucial that a son or daughter inherit the lands, estate, family name, and household deities.

February 15, XV KALENDS MARCH

INUUS

LUPERCALIA

The Lupercalia was an ancient and enigmatic festival finally suppressed in 494 C.E. by Pope Gelasius, who converted it into a Feast of Purification of the Virgin Mary. On the day of the Lupercalia in ancient Rome, special priests (groups of selected young men—Mark Antony was one), met at the Lupercal, a sacred cave where supposedly the she-wolf had cared for Romulus and Remus, legendary founders of Rome. The cave was at the foot of the Palatine Hill and contained a spring and sacred grove. No trace of it has ever been discovered.

After sacrifice of a goat and offerings of sacred cakes of *mola salsa* made by the Vestal Virgins, the high priest smeared the foreheads of young men, the Lupercii, with the blood of a sacrificial goat. Other priests wiped away the blood with wool dipped in milk. At this point in the ritual, the young men had to laugh out loud. The young men cut into strips the skin of the sacrificed goat. Naked except for the strips of the goatskin tied around their waists, the band of young men held a wild drunken feast. In two groups, they ran a circuit from the cave around the city. As they ran, they struck bystanders with thongs of goatskin. Women especially would seek to be ritually touched by the skins. The deity who was honored was the god Inuus, or Goer-In, God of Sexual Intercourse.

ANCIENT RITUAL TO THE HOUSEHOLD DEITIES

When prayers were offered to the household deities, they were spoken in the open air in the atrium or garden, both of which were unroofed. The customary Roman way to pray was with palms upward and hands outstretched. Sacrifice was of incense and firstfruits of grain. Costly animal sacrifice was not necessary. You may simply crown the images of the household deities on your altar with rosemary or myrtle and with pure hands sprinkle *mola salsa* (salted grain).

Offer some incense to your family gods. This is the day that peace-loving Concordia visits your home. Offer bits of food on a plate to the Lares, the household deities, as a token of homage. Now, when the shadows of night invite gentle sleep, fill the wine cup to the brim and say, "Hail to you! Hail to you!" . . . At these words, pour out the wine. (Ovid Fasti 2.630–37)

The search for fertility today has become very scientific and often devoid of the spiritual side, the personal side. It bears its own ritual involving fertility pills, monthly calendars, thermometers, and medical procedures. Fertility rituals in antiquity lacked a scientific approach, yet were grounded in belief, faith, and hope. The ability to conceive was viewed as sacred. Man and woman had to be ritually purified in order to be receptive. The rituals often involved a symbolic act, a transference or channeling of positive fertile energy.

One such fertility ritual, the Lupercalia, held on February 15, was unusual and dated back to prehistoric times. According to the ritual, which was popular in Rome at the beginning of the common era, young naked men, the Lupercii, would race in circles around the streets of Rome purifying and making women fertile with a ceremonial lashing of goatskin thongs. The recipient would then be made pure of all evil spirits that prevented fertility and consequently receptive to impregnation. The antiquity of the rite is apparent in the interconnection between human, animal, and vegetal fertility, as all were enhanced and made pure and receptive to regeneration.

MODERN PURIFICATION RITUAL
BY THE POWER OF THE EARTH

The ancients also purified themselves and possessions by means of fire, water, air, and earth. Purification by fire was done by fumigating or burning herbs and incense; the smoke purified all it touched. Water, often mixed with salt, would be sprinkled on an individual or object. To mix purification of fire and water, a burning stick was taken from the fire, doused with sacred water, and sprinkled on all to be purified. A winnowing fan, one that separates the wheat from the chaff, was used to purify by air. The fan was swung over the head of the person or object to be purified and the bad spirits, just like the chaff, would be separated out and blown away in the air. To purify by earth, an onion dug from the ground was used in antiquity to release pain and to purify. Each layer would be peeled off slowly, and when all the layers were gone, so was the impurity. Tears of healing are a natural and unavoidable part of the process, as I learned.

For our women's group we bought a big juicy red onion from the grocery store. As we passed the onion around the circle, each woman peeled a layer or layers and shared something painful, some part of her life in need of healing. Did we cry! One woman was particularly affected—she was the last in the group to get the onion. As she dug deep with her nails and peeled the layers, pungent juice ran down her hands. She emotionally peeled layers of painful remembrance describing her father's death. In a trancelike state with tears flowing down her face, she kept peeling and talking as she relived cradling him during his dying moments. Then the onion was gone, the peels fallen aside. She released the pain and sobbed. As a group we helped her gently wash her face and hands with lemon-scented soap. This woman shared how meaningful the ritual was for her and how she felt healed and purified for the first time in years. Yet we as observers shared in her deep cleansing and healing. One thought struck each of us: "These old rituals really work!"

Purify Your Lands and Community

Harmful spirits must be banished to ensure fertility and growth in all aspects on one's life. The Romans purified an area by a formal rite called a lustration, in which all bad influences and spirits were banished, thereby making way for the good to come. A lustration was an ordered procession of worshipers moving solemnly around the perimeters of the homes, land, or towns. Priests led chants and prayers along the way, creating a magic circle. At the conclusion of the procession, everything within the boundaries of the circle including people, animals, and land was rendered pure, receptive, and fertile. A sacred circle was cast in February that would last through the yearly cycle.

February 23, VII KALENDS MARCH

TERMINALIA

At the Terminalia, each landowner laid garlands on boundary markers and built an altar nearby. The farmer's wife carried fire from the household hearth, while he chopped wood for the bonfire. A young son threw grain from a basket onto the bonfire at the altar, while the young daughter offered honeycomb. A wine libation was offered as well. It was important that all family members dress in white and maintain silence throughout the ritual. At the conclusion, a feast was held with prayers and songs to honor the boundary and sacred space within. Terminus, spirit of the farmland and its boundaries, was thus appeased and peace was kept between neighbors.

The Terminalia, or Festival of Terminus, God of Boundaries, was originally a farmer's rite. Boundary stones and sacred lines that designated the farmlands were magical spaces and care had to be taken with them. According to Roman myth, when the other rural deities moved inside to temples, Terminus refused to budge from the boundaries of each farm or home. "Oh, Terminus, whether thou art a stone or stump buried in the field, thou too hast been deified since olden days" (Ovid *Fasti* 2.641).

When a boundary was first set up, fruits of the earth, honey, and wine were placed in a hole at the edge of the property and covered with a stone or tree stump. A curse was placed on anyone who moved a boundary stone.

February 13, MOVEABLE RITUAL FROM IDES–KALENDS MARCH

AMBURBIUM

The Amburbium was a ritual to purify the city of Rome and all that lies within. In fact, this festival was an urban counterpart to the rural purification rituals. As a solemn procession of worshipers encircled the city boundaries, they chanted prayers and offered sacrifices. By this lustration, everything inside the limits of the ancient city of Rome was made pure.

February is a quiet month of coming to terms with the past and purifying ourselves through ritual. These publicly celebrated purification rites brought closure to the preparatory period. Once they were completed at the end of February, all was in order. All was purified and made receptive.

Am I wrong, or has the swallow, the herald of the spring, arrived? (Ovid Fasti 2.853)

MARCH

THE MONTH
TO PLANT THE SEED

A PRAYER TO MARS SILVANUS

Father Mars, I pray and beseech you that you may be propitious and well disposed to me, our home and household, for which cause I have ordered the offering of a pig, sheep and ox to be led around my field, my land and my farm, that you may prevent, ward off and avert diseases, visible and invisible, barrenness and waste, accident and bad water, that you would permit the crop and fruit of the earth, the vines and shrubs to wax great and prosper, that you would preserve the shepherds and their flocks in safety and give prosperity and health to me and our house and household. (Cato De Agricultura 142)

Rural Menologia
SUN IN PISCES
31 DAYS
NONES: MARCH 7
DAYLIGHT: 12 HOURS
DARKNESS: 12 HOURS
EQUINOX

The ancient farmers were advised to plow and loosen the soil in the fields and to sow the spring wheat. They were to prune the grapevines and prop them up with wooden stakes. (Menologia)

In March, we come out of our winter shells with a great burst of vitality and energy. These past two months have been quieter periods of intensive inner work. In contrast, March is a month of great activity and external work—a time to assert ourselves and give energy to our efforts. Like the seeds germinating in the moist soil, we have also stored energy inside ourselves. March is a time to express that energy and feel the juices rising after a dormant winter. March is the month to worship the wild within and let ourselves be driven by earthy passion and ambition. We should allow our passionate side a little freedom, and not be afraid to feel the earthy energy of aroused sexuality and sensuality. This energy is truly a creative force—a necessary force.

The month of March, the month to plant seeds, was sacred to Mars, who embodies male sexual energy, because religion and sexuality were closely allied in the Roman world. When we think of Mars, the namesake of this month, we think of a terrifying and bloodthirsty war god. Yet he was a much more complex deity to ancient Roman farmers. Mars Silvanus, or Mavors, his more ancient name, was originally a god of fertility, male sexuality, and vegetation. As such, he was long worshiped in Italy before Rome was founded. This Mars was a god of nature and the wilder regions beyond the city walls; the wolf and woodpecker were sacred to him. In fact, no temple was built to Mars within the city walls of Rome until the period of Augustus (12 B.C.E.), although he did have an open-air altar in the Campus Martius, or Field of Mars. Mars was also a god of protection for the fields and crops, and perhaps this is how he came to acquire a militant identity. We will honor the older Mars Silvanus, the God of Fertility and Abundance.

March is also the month to plant the creative seeds for any endeavor for creation is not restricted to the womb, but can spring from the mind as well. We conceive ideas and thoughts, and so it is appropriate that Mars shares this month with the goddess Minerva. We first associate the Roman Minerva with the Greek goddess Athena and perceive her as a virgin warrior with helmet and spear. Yet, in the earliest Roman times, before Greek influence, Minerva was a clever and astute Goddess of Arts and Crafts. Her very name is derived from the Latin word for "mind," *mens*. Thus, both Mars and Minerva claim this fertile month. Sexuality and creativity are the overriding themes of March.

An amusing and uniquely Roman myth tells the story of Mars and his passion for the virgin Goddess of Arts and Crafts. This virile deity with curly black hair was quite willing to put aside his shield and helmet to woo Minerva. In this myth, he seeks the intervention of Anna Perenna, a wise old crone and deity associated with exuberant sexuality.

How Minerva Tricked Mars

For a long time, Mars had lusted after the goddess Minerva, yet she spurned every one of his advances. "I am a virgin and will remain so," the great goddess declared.

When Anna had been but lately made a goddess, Mars, in frustration, came to her and, taking her aside, said, "You are worshiped in my month. I have joined my season with yours. I have great hope in the service that you can render me. An armed god myself, I have fallen in love with the armed goddess Minerva; I burn and for a long time have nursed this wound. She and I are deities alike in our pursuits; contrive to unite us. That office well befits you, kind old woman." So spoke Mars.

Old Anna duped the god by a false promise and kept him dangling on in foolish hope by dubious delays. When he often pressed her, she said, "I have done your bidding. Minerva is conquered and has yielded at last to your entreaties." The lover Mars believed the old woman and made ready the bridal chamber. To the chamber, the bridal attendants escorted Anna Perenna, dressed like a bride with a veil over her face. As he prepared to kiss his bride, Mars lifted the wedding veil. There stood not the beautiful Minerva, but the old woman Anna Perenna. When Mars suddenly perceived Anna, first shame, then anger moved the god. He had been fooled. The wise old goddess Anna laughed at dear Minerva's lover. Never did anything please Venus more than that. So old jokes are cracked and ribald songs are sung and people love to remember how Minerva and Anna fooled the great god Mars.

→>•<←

This myth describes male sexual energy as seen through the eyes of three female goddesses who represent the three phases in a woman's life: the forthright virgin Minerva, the consummate lover Venus, and the clever crone Anna Perenna. The story describes how Minerva spurns Mars, Anna dupes him, and Venus mocks his unconsummated desires. This is not a story of love, but a tale of male lust. As Mars takes off his armor, he reverts to a god of sexuality and fertility; he is rendered vulnerable by the consuming power of male lust and sexual drive.

Male sexuality is an essential vitality, yet it is one that all women can deal with in their own way and on their own terms, just as these goddesses did. Without succumbing to him or even fearing the all-powerful god Mars, each goddess responded to his testosterone-driven needs on her own terms and in a positive way. Virgin Minerva firmly and with confidence turned away; she just said no! Wise and playful crone Anna tricked and manipulated Mars. The Goddess of Love herself found him amusing and just laughed at his unrequited desire. Interestingly, it was the wiser older woman who enjoyed the sexual game and knew how to diffuse the intensity of male passion. Although aggressive male sexual energy is a natural and necessary aspect of life for all species, women need not feel powerless or victimized and, in fact, do have choices—to thoroughly enjoy the sexual moment, to walk away, to cleverly redirect the advances, or to knowingly laugh.

This myth was appropriately told in March, the month to celebrate the resurgence of spring and sexual energy, when Roman men and women took to the streets shouting, dancing, feasting, and exulting in their sexuality. If this behavior may seem foreign and distant, think of the Mardi Gras or Carnival held today in many countries in early spring. Our own jubilant spring rites would surely please Mars himself.

RITES AND RITUALS OF MARCH

Releasing the Creative Sexual Energy

Just as sap in the dormant trees moves upward, stimulating the burst of colorful blossoms and green leaves, so does March's energy rise within us. We too have been "dormant," or turned inward, for the months of January and February. We have looked at the past, the dead, and the decay;

we have prepared, looked ahead, and purified ourselves. Now is the time to feel that rush of energy moving upward from the earth.

This is the month to let out our strong feelings, those that sometimes overwhelm us, those that have been bottled up inside of us all the dark cold winter. March is the month to honor the male energy in all of us and to move outward with assertion. March is the time to laugh, play, make love, and create. Look around at the natural world. March is not the month to be shy or keep desires and thoughts hidden inside.

Religion and sexuality were closely allied in the Roman world. For many of us today, this is an awkward, uncomfortable, or even blasphemous concept. Yet we humans are part of the natural world; we mate, give birth, live, and die. The moment of birth is awesome and sacred, yet it is also the culmination of the sexual reproductive cycle. Sexuality and spirituality are indeed interrelated.

Male sexuality, the domain of the god Mars, is embodied in the phallus, which represents male creative power. In antiquity, the phallus was viewed as the symbol and the center of male creativity, pleasure, and the unstoppable force of nature and generation.

March 1, KALENDS

MARS

THE SALII

Very ancient rites began on March 1 and lasted the entire month. In fact the entire month of March was special to Mars and his priests, the Salii ("dancers" or "leapers"). The Salii were a group of twenty-four young men of patrician birth whose parents were still alive. They served as special priests during this month and led the processions about Rome in honor of the ancient deity Mars.

What was in oldest times strictly a magical agricultural rite gradually acquired military overtones. Thus, during the later Roman period, the Salii wore archaic military dress with a bronze-belted tunic, a rectangular breastplate, and short military cloak with scarlet stripes and purple borders. They wore cone-shaped helmets and carried swords. In their right hand, they carried a staff or spear and on their left arm wore the sacred figure-eight shield, a copy of an original that supposedly fell from the sky.

The sacred shields were stored throughout the year in the Regia, a building in the Roman Forum. On March 1, the Salii set out on the first of many processions throughout the streets of Rome. As they walked, they would beat their shields, stopping at certain places to sing their ancient hymn to Mavors accompanied by a flute and perform elaborate dances with leaps and bounds. The few words of their song that we have speak to the fertilizing power of the god Mars Gradivus.

In the evening the Salii would retire to a special building, where they would store their shields and dine in great luxury at state expense. They ate so well that the emperor Claudius once left his own banquet to join the Salii, because he thought their food and wine were better.

The rites to Mars took place on the first day of March, his month. It is believed that the original purpose of the ritual was not a war dance with armor, but a dance of noisy display to scare off evil spirits and promote fertility and growth—the figure-eight shield being ceremonial and not functional. The dancing of armed priests may have been to expel evil spirits that had accumulated in the past year throughout the city, especially those that hindered fertility. The weapons of the Salii were not to be used against humans, but evil spirits fearful of loud noises from sacred instruments. The leaps were to simulate the growth of the crops, and the ancient farmers may have measured the expected height of the new crops by the height of the leaps.

The parade must have been colorful, noisy, and entertaining as the leaping priests marched through the streets of ancient Rome in early March. The ritual was also taken seriously. In 190 B.C.E., the famous general Scipio Africanus refused to cross the Hellespont from Greece into modern Turkey to face the attacking Syrian king because the month was March and he was a Salian priest. During the holy days when the sacred shields are carried through the streets of Rome, any Salian priest not present had to remain wherever he was and not travel.

A Day to Honor Women

Although the Kalends of each month were sacred to the goddess Juno, the first day, or the new moon, in March was especially revered. Following a wonderful ancient custom, Roman husbands would pray for the health of their wives and give them presents. An offering was made at the temple of Juno Lucina, where a public banquet was held. Later that evening, the Roman women would entertain their families and friends at banquets. Women also gave presents to other women. The streets of Rome were full of people rushing about delivering presents to mothers, sisters, wives, and friends. Women dressed up in their finest attire on this day. Plautus, a Roman author, speaks of a husband awakened before dawn by his wife who needed money to buy a present for her mother.

March 1, KALENDS

JUNO LUCINA

MATRONALIA

The Matronalia, the Festival to Women, honoring Juno Lucina, was celebrated on the Kalends, or first day of March. On that day, the Vestal Virgins would enter the sacred grove of trees and hang offerings of their hair on the oldest tree. The rites to Juno Lucina at her temple were strictly for women; men were forbidden.

Juno Lucina is the Goddess of Women and Childbirth, and her epithet comes from the Latin *lux*, "light." Hence, she presided over the birth of the baby and the child's first view of light. It was ruled by the state that for every birth of a baby a coin should be deposited in the temple of Juno Lucina as a way to thank the goddess and keep track of the growing population as well. It was the custom for pregnant women who worshiped Juno Lucina to unbind their hair and untie any knots in their clothing; for nothing restricting, even symbolically, should be allowed to hamper a safe delivery.

MODERN RITUAL OF FIRST LIGHT

First and foremost this month, we honor women and motherhood. Reestablish the custom of sharing presents with women on the first day of March.

- Make sure that flowers are a part of your day; buy some or pick some if they are already blooming.
- Place bouquets of sweet-smelling, colorful flowers on your desk or table.
- Be bold and "garland your hair with flowers" as the Roman women did to honor Juno the Light Bringer.
- This is also a day to honor children, who received small gifts in antiquity. Pay special attention to the young people in your life—it is their day too and they need to see some light!

PRAYER TO LUCINA

Child of Latona... lady of mountains and green woods, and sequestered glens and sounding rivers, thou art called Juno Lucina by mothers in pain of labor, thou are called mighty Trivia and Luna with counterfeit light. Thou Goddess, measures out by monthly course the circuit of the year and fillest full with goodly fruits the rustic home of the farmer. (Catullus *Poem 34*)

> *Bring flowers to the Goddess, Juno Lucina;*
> *She takes delight in flowering plants.*

> *Wear garlands of delicate flowers in your hair for her.*
> *Say to her, "You have opened our eyes to the light. Oh, Juno Lucina.*
> *Hear the prayers of women in labor."*
> *If you are pregnant, let down your hair and do not bind it.*
> *Pray to Juno Lucina for an easy and safe delivery.*
>   *(Ovid Fasti 3.255–65)*

The Sacred and the Obscene

Anna Perenna was an old crone deity of the yearly cycle often associated with the full moon—the Ides of March. In fact, in earliest times, March was the first month of the new year. The festival held to Anna Perenna involved private rituals at the household altar and a public rite celebrated in her sacred grove along the Tiber River. This was a ribald and uninhibited event.

March 15, IDES

ANNA PERENNA

Anna Perenna was a female deity who oversaw the continuity from one year to the next. She was depicted as an old woman and honored on the Ides of March.

Ovid describes this day in honor of Anna Perenna as a joyous celebration where men and women set up tents or constructed simple grass huts near her sacred grove. There was a great deal of drinking, dancing, and partying. The idea was to drink as many cups of wine to Anna as the number of years you wished to live. Popular and obscene songs were sung as couples withdrew for private celebrations of the sexuality of the season. Martial quips that Anna's grove "delights in virgin blood." The association with fertility is easy to see. This particular rite turned into a glorious outdoor party with wine, dancing, and lewd stories; many couples retired to their leafy huts in the sacred grove.

The sexuality was playful, flirtatious, and bawdy. Laughter was a key element in the worship of Anna Perenna. Many of us have a difficult time with that notion. "The very idea of sexuality as sacred, and more specifically, obscenity as an aspect of sacred sexuality, is vital to the wildish nature. . . . In laughter, a woman can begin to really breathe, and when she does this, she might begin to feel unsanctioned feelings" (Pinkola Estés, 335–36). It is older goddesses like Anna Perenna who can show us how to roar with bawdy laughter and to loosen those inhibitions that grip and tighten us inside. It is difficult with Anna nearby to repress the laugh that comes from deep within the belly. Extroverted behavior is called for this month.

Carnevale takes place in Italy during the month of February, yet in spirit it is more like the raucous celebrations held in March in ancient Rome. Though each modern Italian town retains its own special traditions and foods to celebrate the festive season, the end of Carnevale is often a time of masked balls, parades, and grand feasts. In the small town of Ivrea, Carnevale is celebrated with a fierce battle using oranges. On the battlefield, which covers an area the size of five town plazas, two teams of two to three hundred "soldiers" battle with other fighters passing by on horse-drawn carts. The young men hurl oranges at each other in mock battle with juice and pulp splattering everyone. Solely for this purpose, a train holding sixty tons of blood oranges arrives from Sicily at Carnevale time. This display of aggressive male energy should please Mars himself.

In this same small town, the end of Carnevale is marked by a spectacular display of light. Poles as tall as trees are sunk into the earth and encircled with garlands of heather and juniper. At nightfall in the central plaza, young boys ignite the garlands with their torches and the flames shoot to the very top of the poles. A final feast is held and Carnevale in Ivrea is over. Yet what a feast it is, with 1,200 pounds of fish and 175 pounds of onions, 300 quarts of lasagna, and of course 250 liters of wine and polenta to feed an army. The emperor Claudius was known to drop in on similar banquets in ancient Rome during the month of March (Field, 34–50).

MODERN RITUAL TO FEEL THE ENERGY, TO ENERGIZE

It would be wonderful to take part in a community ritual like Carnevale, yet even a smaller gathering of friends for a party with wine, music, feasting, and dancing will serve the purpose. It does feel good to be with other people, to laugh, and be boisterous. Here, special recipes to help you celebrate Carnevale.

ROAST LAMB

Let us roast the lamb adding an ounce of pepper, a little ginger, parsley, and a spoonful of olive oil. (Apicius *De Re Coquinaria* 8.6.8)

3 pounds leg of lamb
1 tablespoon freshly ground black pepper
1/2 teaspoon ground ginger
3 tablespoons chopped parsley
2 tablespoons olive oil
salt

SAUCE
4 tablespoons olive oil
1 cup red wine
10 dried dates, chopped and mashed
2 tablespoons honey
salt and pepper, to taste

Mix ingredients and rub over the lamb. Roast at 350 degrees for 20 to 30 minutes per pound. Let cool when done.

Prepare sauce. Place ingredients in a saucepan, and bring to a boil. Reduce slightly. You may thicken the sauce with cornstarch. Serve with the lamb.

EPITYRUM OLIVE SPREAD

Recipe for a relish of green, ripe, and black olives. Remove the pit from green, ripe, and black olives, and proceed as follows: chop the flesh and add oil, vinegar, coriander, cumin, fennel, rue, and mint. Put them in an earthenware dish, cover them with oil and serve. (Cato *De Agricultura* 119)

12 ounces pitted black olives
pinch of coriander seeds
pinch of cumin
pinch of fennel

pinch of rue (hard to find, not to worry)
pinch of mint
olive oil as needed
vinegar as needed

Combine herbs and pitted olives in a food processor. Gradually add oil and vinegar and process for 1 minute. Put epityrum in a glass jar and cover with olive oil. Store in refrigerator. Keep on hand for hors d'oeuvres and to spread on your freshly baked bread.

Fertility and the Vine

The week of the full moon was also the time for the rites to Liber, the Liberalia. On this day, older women acted as priestesses of Liber, an old Italic god of fertility and especially of the vine, who was later associated with Bacchus and Dionysus. On the day of the Liberalia, these women crowned themselves with wreaths of ivy and set up stands on street corners throughout ancient Rome. Here, they had small portable altars and would offer sacrifice to Liber at the request of any passerby. The common offering was a rich honey cake.

March 17, XVI KALENDS APRIL

LIBER

LIBERALIA

The Liberalia was primarily a rustic festival celebrated in the countryside by farmers, where Liber presided over the seed of men (male semen). In small farming towns throughout Italy, a phallus was carried on a cart around the countryside accompanied by a procession of people singing obscene songs. The phallus was taken finally into the center of town, where it was placed for the month of March. At Lavinium, a virtuous woman was assigned to lay a wreath on the phallus. This was done to promote fertility and ensure a good season for the crops. The close bond between sexuality and spirituality is not difficult to perceive in this rite. After all, this is the theme of March.

On March 17, two days after the full moon, on the day sacred to Bacchus or Liber, rites were publicly held to honor young men. This was the day that Roman youths would officially receive the togas of manhood and be cheered on by friends and family. It does seem fitting that the public honor and recognizes young male energy in mid-March. What a vibrant time!

MODERN RITUAL TO TASTE THE WINE

Honor the Liberalia and the god Bacchus by tasting his gift of the vine. This is a good time to have a wine tasting. Or try the Roman drink mulsum, a mixture of honey and wine:

HONEYED MULSUM-WINE

$1/2$ cup honey
pinch ground allspice
1 bottle dry white wine

Place the honey together with $1/4$ cup of the wine in a pan. Warm slowly to let the honey dissolve. Add a pinch of ground allspice. Slowly add the remaining bottle of wine. Stir well. Chill before serving.

Creativity of the Mind: A Sacred Process

Until now we have focused on sexuality and procreation. Minerva reminds us that we can create from the mind as well as the womb. She is in origin an old Italic goddess of crafts and handiwork. She is clever and nimble in thought, a goddess of knowledge, arts, and crafts, "a goddess of a thousands works."

March 19–23, XIV–IX KALENDS APRIL

MINERVA

GREATER QUINQUATRUS

The festival to Minerva lasted five days and was called the Greater Quinquatrus. The first day of the festival, just after the Ides, was called an *artificium dies,* or "day of the arts." On this day, doctors, teachers, and students also sacrificed to Minerva, especially at her temple on the Aventine.

Let girls learn how to card the wool and work the distaffs. Minerva also teaches us how to weave on the upright loom warp with a shuttle. She tightens the loose threads with a comb. Worship her, you who want to remove stains from your clothes. Worship her, you who dye the wool in large bronze kettles. Cherish her, you who carve and sculpt in stone, or you who paint brightly colored pictures. Minerva is the Goddess of a thousand works. Surely, she is the Goddess of poetry as well. (Ovid *Fasti* 3.811–34)

THE COMPETITION OF MINERVA AND ARACHNE

In the myth, Minerva accepts the young girl's challenge to competition in this colorful passage on the art of weaving:

> They both set up the looms in different places without delay and they stretch the fine warp upon them. The web is bound upon the beam, the reed separates the threads of the warp, the woof is threaded through them by the sharp shuttles which their busy fingers ply, and when shot though the threads of the warp, the notched teeth of the hammering slay beat into place. They sped on the work with their mantles close girt about their breasts and move back and forth their well-trained hands, their eager zeal beguiling their toil. There are inwoven the purple threads dyed in Tyrian kettles and lighter colors insensibly shading off from these. As when after a storm of rain the sun's rays strike through, and a rainbow with its huge curve stains the wide sky, though a thousand different colors shine in it, the eye cannot detect the change from each one to the next; so like appear the adjacent colors, but the extreme are plainly different. There too they weave in pliant threads of gold and trace in the weft some ancient tale. (Ovid Metamorphosis 6.54–69, LCL)

According to the myth, golden-haired Minerva became so indignant at the boastful girl that she sprinkled Arachne with an herb, transforming her boastful girl into a spider forever weaving her web.

The latter part of March was the time to celebrate the Greater Quin-quatrus, usually March 19 and the four next days. This festival was special to Minerva not in her warlike guise, but as the Goddess of the Arts. For indeed, creativity comes from the mind and soul as well as the womb, and prayers for fertile ideas bear equal weight during this month of March. The festival was also sacred to Mars, as the Salii again danced this day.

MODERN RITUAL TO HONOR YOUR CREATIVE SELF

This month of March is not a time to feel shy or restrained. Be creative—try some artistic or creative project. This is the time to get in touch with your creative ideas and express them outwardly through dance, painting, music, writing, or other arts.

- Purchase and work with some soft soapstone and tools for carving small figurines.
- Buy pads of white paper and set time aside for writing and journaling.
- Select a special dress pattern with luxurious material to sew.
- Choose your favorite colors and patterns, and work a piece of needlepoint.
- Take a class in painting or dance or poetry.
- Explore and identify your own creative path. It is the creative spirit and drive to express yourself through art or craft that is the gift of the goddess Minerva. Indeed, talent is a goddess-given gift—given to each of us in different ways.

March now draws to an end. Mars is honored this month with one of the oldest prayers in Roman religion.

HYMN TO MAVORS (MARS)

Oh! Help us, ye Household Gods! Oh! Help us, ye Household Gods! Oh!
  Help us, ye Household Gods!
And let not bane and bale, O Marmor (Mars or Mavors), assail more folk!
  And let not bane and bale, O Marmor (Mars or Mavors), assail more folk!
  And let not bane and bale, O Marmor (Mars or Mavors), assail more folk!

Be full satisfied, fierce Mars. Leap the threshold! Halt! Beat the ground! Be full satisfied, fierce Mars. Leap the threshold! Halt! Beat the ground! Be full satisfied, fierce Mars. Leap the threshold! Halt! Beat the ground!

By turns address ye all the Half-Gods. By turns address ye all the Half-Gods. By turns address ye all the Half-Gods.

Oh! Help us, Marmor! Oh! Help us, Marmor! Oh! Help us, Marmor! Bound, bound and bound again, bound and bound again! (CIL VI 2104 LCL)

APRIL

THE MONTH
TO CONCEIVE

It is said that April was named for the open [apertum] season,
Because spring opens all things and
The sharp frost bound cold gives way,
The soil thaws and is easily worked.
Venus lays claim to this month.
This most deserving goddess governs the entire world.
This queen rules a kingdom second to none.
(Ovid Fasti 4.87–130 LCL)

Rural Menologia
SUN IN ARIES
NONES: APRIL 5
30 DAYS
DAYLIGHT: $13^{1}/_{2}$ HOURS
DARKNESS: $10^{1}/_{2}$ HOURS

⟶⟩⟩•⟨⟨⟵

Ancient farmers were advised to weed the crops, break the ground with oxen pulling the plow, cut the willows, fence in the meadows, and plant and tend the olive trees. (Menologia)

April is the most sensual of months, a time to sink down into the new grass and open all of our senses to the natural world. This gentle month warms both our bodies and spirits. What a heady rush to the senses this month, with the sounds of songbirds outside our window heralding dawn's rosy return; the sweet fragrance of lilacs and roses beginning to bloom; the overwhelming splash of yellow forsythia, pink, red, and purple azaleas, snowy white blossoms on the fruit trees; the welcoming feel of sunlight on bare skin; the taste of spring.

The wild and erratic month of March is gone. Growth is all around us and can't be denied. We succumb to the alluring and sensual qualities of the earth—of female sexuality. We lie exposed, open, and receptive to the sensual flow oozing out of the natural world, washing over us wave after wave. We are at one with the animals and flowers; we respond as they do. We can do little else! As all living things, we fall under the power of the goddess Venus. April is ruled by Venus and appropriately so!

Venus, the goddess we honor and whose statue we adorn this month, is an earthy deity—she is the Creatrix of all, she is Nature incarnate. And, as the Roman poet Lucretius writes, "Throughout seas and mountains and sweeping torrents, and the leafy dwellings of birds and lush green plains, the Goddess Venus strikes soft love into the breasts of all creatures. She cause them to be lustful, and reproduce" (*De Rerum Natura* 1.1–15 LCL). No species in heaven, on the earth, or under the sea would exist without her. This goddess is no mindless and simple seductress, the product of male imagination and fantasy, as Venus has been popularly portrayed over the centuries. The awesome goddess we worship in April is much more complex. Her roots go deep into primordial soil—her power is found in the direct, seamless, and accessible presence of nature. She is all-encompassing as Giver of Life and source of regenerative female energy so intimately connected with the earth, the natural world. Sexuality and sensuality are the tools of Venus, and she employs them at her will. Sexual desire is a goddess-sent gift, as the young sculptor Pygmalion discovered.

Pygmalion

The people living in the town of Amanthus, on the island of Cyprus, had turned away from the goddess Venus. They had defiled her altars with blood sacrifice and even dared to deny her divinity.

"I shall leave this place," vowed Venus, "and abandon all people living on Cyprus." Yet the goddess paused. "Why should I leave the island that I love so well and where I was born from the waters? How can I turn my back on the innocent people who tend my altars and honor my presence? Instead, I will punish only the impious people not with death or exile, but by transformation. I will make the godless men into bulls and the unfaithful women into prostitutes. If they cannot love me, then as women, they have little love of themselves."

Because of their impiety toward Venus, the women of Amanthus were the first to prostitute their souls and their bodies. Having been rejected, the goddess withdrew and, as a result, the women lost their modesty, self-respect, and self-love. They became bitter, cold, and critical. Their inner beauty vanished and they turned ugly. As they lost the power to feel good about themselves, the women who doubted the goddess lost the ability to blush, and the blood in their faces hardened like their hearts. Soon the women became so heartless and cold they were transformed into stones.

The sight of these hardened, loveless women disgusted the sculptor Pygmalion. He cherished female beauty and sensuality, yet could not find a wife. And so he lived without a partner, avoiding all women. Yet in his dreams he envisioned the perfect woman, the perfect female body. And with wondrous artistic gift, he carved an ivory figure more lovely than any woman born. And so he had made a woman in the likeness of Venus herself, and he fell deeply in love.

She seemed so real, he thought, that she may even move her limbs and reach out to touch him. His desire was driving him mad. Pygmalion became obsessed with this female beauty. He tried to touch the skin to see if it was ivory or flesh. He kissed the female form and thought that his kisses were returned. He spoke to the cold white female shape in his studio. He grasped her wrist, hoping that his fingers would sink into flesh, fearful that he would leave a bruise.

Pygmalion brought gifts pleasing to women, shells and smooth pebbles for jewelry, many-hued flowers, lilies, and drops of amber. He clothed her with robes, put gems on her fingers, and placed a long gold neck-lace around her neck. Pearls hung from her ears and a chain of pearls adorned her breast. All of these gifts were beautiful, yet not as beautiful as the naked female body itself.

Soon, the day sacred to Venus arrived. All Cyprus thronged to cele-brate the great goddess. Altars smoked with incense to the goddess. Pygmalion, too, brought a gift to the altar of Venus and stood, hesitating to pray. "O you, Venus, can give all things, I pray to have as my wife..." He faltered with his choice of words. "One like my ivory maid."

But Golden Venus was herself present at the festival, and she knew the meaning of the prayer. The awesome goddess drew near and as she did, the altars blazed alive with her presence, sending flares high into the sky three times.

Pygmalion hastened home and gently kissed his ivory woman. She seemed warm to his touch. He kissed her again and with his hands touched her arm. The ivory grew soft to his touch, and its hardness van-ished; it yielded to his fingers just as wax grows warm under the sun and becomes malleable. The lover stood amazed and dumbstruck. Pygmalion rejoiced, yet he still had his doubts, fearing he was mistaken or truly gone mad. He tried again with his hand. Yes, it was real flesh! The veins were pulsing beneath his testing fingers. Then did the sculp-tor from Cyprus pour out copious thanks to the goddess Venus. The young woman felt the kisses and blushed, opening her eyes for the first time to see the light of the sky and her lover together; for she returned his love at once. The goddess graced the marriage she had so cleverly arranged. And when the tenth month had brought her crescent moon to the full, a daughter was born to them, and they called her Paphos.

This myth underscores the ability of the goddess to bring female beauty and sensuality to life. As the myth conveys, the essence of living female beauty is not what appears on the outside alone, but what is goddess-born from within. It is simplistic and even harmful to view femi-ninity as possessed only by beautiful model-like women and perfectly sculpted statues. The magic Venus bestows upon the cold ivory statue is the same magic that awaits all women who are receptive to her touch.

We each carry inside a very primal and personal wish that does not diminish with age. It is the wish to be attractive, to be sought after, to be desired. We want to be beautiful as reflected in our own eyes and the eyes of our lovers! Yet, how often are we critical and judgmental of our appearance and our beauty. When we shed our protective clothing and stand naked before a mirror, more often than not our first thoughts are critical ones. We immediately berate ourselves, "I am too fat. Why didn't I stick to that exercise program or say no to that rich dessert last night? My hips are too broad, my breasts are no longer firm, my face is getting wrinkled. How can I ever look like those slender fashion models?"

Take heart and learn from the story of Venus and Pygmalion that true female beauty is a gift of the goddess Venus, and this gift is more than skin deep. We are surrounded today with commercial images in magazines, movies, and on television of thin, young women who set a standard for female beauty—a standard that we are all encouraged to equal. The quest for physical beauty can be superficial. In the myth, Pygmalion, a man, also defines beauty, by sculpting the "perfect woman." Although she is beautiful, the statue remains lifeless, a cold piece of ivory that obsesses the young sculptor and slowly drives him mad. He cannot enliven her; he can only adore her. This statue of the "perfect woman" and the image of femininity only comes to fulfillment with the gift of life brought by the touch of a goddess. At once, the cold ivory warms from within, and the veins pulse blood.

Venus resides within us, and we must have faith in her. When the women of Amanthus turned against Venus, they really denied the goddess-given innate feminine qualities. They degraded and prostituted themselves and could no longer perceive their own beauty, their softness and female sensuality. They became hard and ugly and turned into stones, while the ivory statue of Pygmalion came to life and love. Pygmalion's beautiful lover is never named in the myth, as she represents each of us. She bears each of our names.

We possess the goddess-given power to respond to our beautiful sensual selves. We only need to have faith in our true beauty. Listen closely, as the goddess within instructs. "You are a beautiful, sensual person. Bathe in heavenly sweet-smelling oils, put on alluring clothes, don golden shining earrings, and encircle your soft throat with lovely necklaces." This sensual month of April, invoke the goddess of female sexuality and sensuality. Be touched by Venus!

RITES AND RITUALS OF APRIL

Honor Female Sexuality

This is the month to honor female sexuality and sensuality, and we can do so in many ways. We can pay attention to the things that arouse or excite our senses, the perfume of a budding lilac, the shading of a pink rose, the sound of a flute, the sensation of warm water in a bubble bath. Whatever heightens our awareness to the world of senses should be pursued this month. April is the time for lovemaking.

April 1, KALENDS

V E N U S

VENERALIA

Every year on the Kalends of April, the women of Rome took down the cult statue of Venus and gave it a good bath.

> Do you worship the goddess, Latin wives, old and young and you who may not dress like respectable women. Take off the golden necklaces from the marble neck of the goddess, take off her decorations. The goddess must be washed from top to toe. Then dry her neck and restore to it her golden necklaces; now give her other flowers, now give her fresh roses. You, too, she herself bids bathe under the green myrtle, and there is a certain reason for her command. Naked she was drying on the shore her dripping locks when the satyrs, a wanton group, spied the goddess. She perceived it and screened her body with myrtle branches. This kept her safe, so she demands you repeat it. . . . Don't hesitate to take a dose of poppy crushed in snowy-white milk with honey dripping from the comb. When her passionate husband first led Venus to bed, she drank this. (Ovid *Fasti* 4.135–45)

It was the custom on this day for Roman women (just the prostitutes, if you believe Ovid) wearing myrtle wreaths to bathe in the men's public baths because "in them men exposed that part of their body by which the favor of women is sought. . . . All women strip when they enter that place [the baths] and every blemish is plain to see. Fortuna [or Venus] conceals the blemish and hides it from the men. She does this for a little incense in return" (Ovid *Fasti* 4.149–53).

Walking down a crowded city street or sitting in a park, we may look up to see a man or woman and sense an attraction. Our breath is a little bit shorter and our gaze a little bit longer. We may turn our eyes to follow the person, but only for a second. Then we go about our day. Venus Verticordia, or Heart Turner, was nearby. Venus does her job safeguarding the generations and overseeing regeneration of all species. Her secret tool is sexual attraction. This feeling hits us below the belt (for this is not a rational thing), and we find it difficult to predict or control. We do, however, have power over our subsequent actions. The feeling of sexual attraction was not considered ungodly or sinful by the ancients. Quite the opposite, for we are part of the sacred regenerative natural cycle. Remember, it is a goddess who instills this feeling, and she deserves to be honored.

The Veneralia was celebrated on the Kalends of April, a rite to Venus the Heart Turner. The goddess Fortuna Virilis was also honored on this day; she has power over women and their dealings with men—those fateful relationships. On this day Roman women of all classes celebrated their sexuality and sought support from Venus herself. This was a day to entertain friends for dinner after attending the rituals at the temple.

It is time to bare ourselves and see how beautiful we really are. Although Roman women had their own separate public bathing complexes, on April 1, some would boldly invade those baths reserved for men. But before doing so, they prayed to Venus to hide any blemishes from male view. And Venus would do this in exchange for a little incense at the altar. Then, with blemishes hidden, en masse, they would disrobe and jump in the *frigidarium* (cool swimming pool) or take a hot sauna in the *caldarium* as male customers looked on.

This was also the day when the women would take Venus's statue down from her place in the temple and give her a good bath, taking off her gold jewelry, washing her from head to toe, and putting fresh roses in her hair. Venus values the importance of feeling sexually attractive. She relishes it!

MODERN RITUAL TO HONOR FEMALE SENSUALITY AND BEAUTY

Venus recommends that all women bathe on this day, preferably under a myrtle bush, her sacred white flower. Finding a secluded myrtle bush is not so easy; however, touching your body, rubbing perfumed oils into your skin, and seeing your true beauty naked are very healing acts. The goddess Venus surely saw her own beauty and can guide you in recognizing your own.

How easy it is to become overly critical of our bodies as we seek some form of perfection. Pray to her to hide whatever blemish or imperfection your self-scrutiny brings to light. Then look in the mirror and see how beautiful you really are! Venus helps us accept and love ourselves. Imagine having the confidence to undress publicly in the men's baths. Faith and belief in Venus were all that was necessary for these Roman women on April 1. Believing in your beauty is the key—that is easy this month, as everything is full of beauty in April!

Remember, Venus is especially fond of rose, myrtle, and mint, and this is her month.

- Try a rose petal bath. Gather yellow, pink, or deep red roses from your garden or purchase them at the florist. Sprinkle about two cups of petals over the warm water of your bath and add a few drops of rose oil. Sink down into your rose strewn bath and luxuriate in a very sensual experience.
- Rosewater, the favorite of Venus, is a simple scent that women have enjoyed for millennia. Make your own rosewater scent; it isn't too difficult. Mix freshly gathered rose petals together with distilled water and heat slowly. Pour in a glass vial to store. Remember, the scent of roses is a sign that Venus is nearby.
- Place myrtle branches with their small white flowers around your bathtub in small vases and feel like a goddess.

The Sacred Rebirth

After months of darkness, we may think that it will never happen again. And then in April, it does. Spring arrives and just as the grasses push through the moist earth seeking the sunlight, our spirits and souls too rise up. April is the month to celebrate the "sacred rebirth," the return of spring and the abundant plant life. This month, Christians celebrate "The Coming" with Easter services. In ancient Rome, the worship of two great mother goddesses, Magna Mater and Ceres, also celebrated rebirth and culminated in April rituals.

April 4–10, I Nones–IV Ides

MAGNA MATER

MEGALESIA

The cult of the Great Mother Cybele (Magna Mater, as the Romans knew her) was introduced into Rome from Phrygia in 204 B.C.E. A sacred black stone was placed in a temple on the Palatine Hill and dedicated to the goddess on April 10, 191 B.C.E. The sacred black stone was described as very small and set into a silver image of the goddess in place of her face. The Roman Magna Mater may have been the inspiration for the Black Madonna.

The ceremony of the Megalesia began by an offering of a dish of herbs at the temple of Magna Mater. The reason of offering simple herbs is because "people of old are reported to have subsisted on pure milk and such herbs as the earth bore of its free will. White cheese is mixed with pounded herbs, that the ancient goddess may know the ancient foods"(Ovid *Fasti* 4.367–73).

MODERN RITUAL TO HONOR REBIRTH AND THE FEMININE

Eggs contain the essence of new life and have represented the spirit of rebirth and the spirit of Ceres and the Great Mother since prehistoric times. Eggs are always part of the Easter celebration, especially in southern Italy today, where they are baked into cakes. In one Italian town, eggs were once set in doll-shaped breads as breasts; in Sardinia, the Easter bread was in the form of a snake wrapped around a bright red hard-boiled egg. (Field, 423–27)

- Using a favorite bread recipe, shape the bread into a creative form and insert whole raw eggs in the shell into the dough. As the raw dough and eggs cook, they are transformed into a delectable gift of the goddess.

The rites of Magna Mater were celebrated by her own eunuch priests, the Galli, sometime during March, but these rites, involving frenzy, violence, and self-mutilation, remained perverse and foreign to most Romans. The four-day rites of the Galli, however, cut to the core of the myth of Attis and his rebirth. In myth, Attis, beloved of Magna Mater, castrated himself, died, and was reborn. Male consort of the Great Mother, he was a vegetation god who returned every spring.

Roman citizens were not allowed to walk in the March procession, take part in the rites, or join the priesthood of Magna Mater, "so great is the aversion of the Romans to all undue display that is lacking in decorum" (Dionysus of Halicarnassus 2.19.4). Instead, they initiated a more moderate Romanized annual festival to Cybele, or Magna Mater, the Megalesia, which began on April 4. The April Megalesia was a cheerful, festive, and raucous ritual of parties and theatrical events. The Megalesia was a time for giving and attending dinner parties and visiting friends. In fact, the banquets became so lavish that the Senate in 161 B.C.E. by decree put a monetary limit on the amount a host could spend for a dinner party in addition to vegetables, bread, and wine, with no foreign wines allowed. The silverware could not weigh more than 120 lbs.

MODERN RITUAL TO HONOR THE GREAT MOTHER

Celebrate the festival of Magna Mater with a dinner party and use your best china and silver (not over 120 lbs., though).

- Decorate with bright spring colors—yellows or greens with white candles. Begin the feast as the Romans did, with an herb and cheese appetizer.
- Select the freshest vegetables of spring to serve, possibly asparagus or artichokes, or tiny new potatoes.
- Make the menu rich and indulgent with Parthian Chicken as a main course.

PARTHIAN CHICKEN

This modern adaptation is derived from the cookbook by the Roman chef Apicius. (De Re Coquinaria 6.9.2) It comes from Parthia, one of the easternmost provinces of the Roman Empire.

1 chicken	2 teaspoons salt
$^1/_2$ teaspoon ground black pepper	2 gloves garlic
$^1/_2$ cup chopped parsley	water
pinch of caraway seeds	

Cut the chicken into pieces. Dissolve the salt in 4 tablespoons of water. Mix in a blender the pepper, parsley, caraway seeds, and salt dissolved in water. Add and blend the two cloves of garlic. Add a little more water if necessary. Put the chicken in an earthenware "Roman" pot, and pour the blended sauce over the chicken. Cover and bake in a 450-degree oven until tender (approximately 1 hour and 20 minutes).

Another Great Mother goddess, Ceres, was honored during these April days with rituals and games. Just as the rite to Magna Mater, the Megalesia, ended, the ritual to Ceres, the Cerialia, began. It lasted from April 12 to 19, or five days during the full moon. Ceres is the Grain Goddess. Her name comes from the Latin word *creare*, "to grow," and the full moon of April is the time for rebirth and growth.

April 12–19, III IDES–XIII KALENDS MAY

C E R E S

CERIALIA

The Cerialia began just as the Megalesia ended, with horse races and games to celebrate both. This celebration was in honor of the goddess Ceres and her joy at the return of her daughter Persephone.

> There is no need to declare the reason; the bounty and the services of the goddess are manifest. The bread of the first mortals consisted of the green herbs which the earth yielded without solicitation; and now they plucked the living grass from the turf, and now the tender leaves of the tree-tops furnished a feast. Afterwards, the acorn became known and the sturdy oak afforded a splendid bounty. Ceres was the first who invited man to better sustenance and exchanged acorns for more useful food. She forced bulls to yield their neck to the yoke; then for the first time did the upturned soil behold the sun. Copper was now held in esteem; iron ore still lay concealed; ah, would that it had been hidden forever! [Weapons were made of iron.] Ceres delights in peace; and you farmer, pray for perpetual peace and a peaceful leader. You may give the goddess Ceres some spelt, and the compliment of spurting salt and grains of incense on old hearths; and if there is no incense kindle resin torches. Good Ceres is content with little, if that little be but pure. (Ovid *Fasti* 4.395–415 LCL)

White was the color to be worn at the festival to Ceres—no dark and somber colors for this month. Persephone returns and the earth is in celebration, decked out in a rainbow of colors to welcome the daughter back. In the countryside, her ritual was conducted on April 19. When spring came, the country folk worshiped Ceres with offerings of milk, honey, and wine.

Persephone, the daughter of Ceres, who dwells in the underworld for the winter months, now returns. Persephone is reunited with her mother, Ceres, and the sacred bond between mother and daughter is renewed this month. These rites of the April Cerialia are only half of the story, the joyous part when all is restored. September bears the other half, the grief and mourning, when the greater rites to Ceres and her daughter Persephone, the Eleusinian Mysteries, are held.

MODERN MOTHER AND DAUGHTER RITUAL

Find an old picture of yourself taken when you were the age that your daughter is now. Share the photo with your daughter. As you do, think back to that time so many years ago. Recall your life at that age. What career had you thought of? Who were your friends? What were your values and ideals? What were your dreams?

Then share a picture of yourself today, one taken recently, discuss the very positive things that you do, and describe the person you have become. Could you perhaps suggest a change in your life that you would like to bring about? Could those old childhood dreams be resurrected? Allow your daughter to share her dreams and wishes with you. Listen to her and love her. Feeling close to your daughter is appropriate anytime. Yet a reaffirmation of a mother's love for a daughter and a daughter's for her mother is natural in April.

The Sacred and Fertile Earth

The last half of April was the time to celebrate Terra Mater, Mother Earth, and all her bounty with four agricultural festivals: the Fordicidia, the Parilia, the Vinalia, and the Robigalia. Rituals centering on the goddesses closely associated with growth and fertility were held after the full moon, the Ides, of April. It was always crucial to pray to Ceres, Pales, Venus, and Robiga as well as numerous other spirits for good growth, bountiful crops, and a successful vintage.

April 15, XVI KALENDS MAY

F O R D I C I D I A

The Fordicidia was a very old festival to ensure fertility of the land and the herds. A pregnant cow bearing a calf *(forda)* was sacrificed to Terra Mater, or Mother Earth. The unborn calf was offered for sacrifice by the Vestal Virgins, who kept the ashes for use at the Parilia days later. The fertility of the cow was to be preserved through the ashes of the calf and returned to the fields to the grain and back to the womb of the earth.

April 21, X KALENDS MAY

P A L E S

PARILIA

The Parilia was an ancient rite to purify the flocks held in honor of the somewhat mysterious deity Pales. Ovid describes this ritual to the goddess Pales, which must include leaping three times over a bonfire fueled by the ashes of the unborn calf and beanstalks while sprinkling water on oneself with a laurel branch.

> Shepherd, do purify your well-fed sheep at twilight; first sprinkle the ground with water and sweep it with a broom. Deck the sheepfold with leaves and branches fastened to it; adorn the door and cover it with a long garland. Make blue smoke with pure sulphur and let the sheep touched with the smoking sulphur bleat. Burn wood of male olives and vine and let the singed laurel crackle in the middle of the hearth. And let a basket of millet accompany cakes of millet; the rural goddess [Pales] particularly delights in that food. Offer food and a pail of milk, such as she loves, and when the food is cut up, pray to rustic Pales, offering warm milk to her. Say, "Oh, Pales, take care of my farm and the farm animals. Ward off evil from the stalls, and let harm flee away. If I have offended you unknowingly, if my pruning shear has cut down a sacred tree, if I have entered a sacred grove without knowledge, do not count it against me. Forgive me!

85

Goddess Pales, appease the sacred springs and their water nymphs. Drive away disease from my household. Avert hunger. Let grass and leaves and trees be plentiful and water both for washing and drinking. May my prayer be granted, and we will make great cakes for Pales every year on this day."

With these words, the goddess will be propitiated. Pronounce this prayer four times, facing the east, and wash your hands in the dew. Offer pure white milk. Build bonfires of crackling straw, and leap over them with nimble feet. (Ovid *Fasti* 4.735–80)

Roman farmers always took a very practical approach to religion. Harm to their families, lands, herds, and crops involved the presence of bad spirits, powers that had not been placated or appeased. Although many were nameless, some carried the names of their functions or were simply called Indigetes, or "Invoked Spirits." These numerous spirits oversaw all aspects of life from birth to death. When sacrificing to Ceres, at least twelve of these spirits had to be invoked including Vervactor, the "spirit who oversaw ploughing," and Promitor, the "spirit who oversaw the sowing." Other deities such as Verminus, the "spirit who protected cattle against worms," were also honored.

April 23, VIII Kalends May

VENUS

VINALIA

The Vinalia was one of two wine festivals (the other was held in August). In April, eight days before the new moon, wine of the previous year was opened, offering to Jupiter was made, and the wine was tasted for the first time. This was a special day for courtesans and prostitutes. "Offer incense and pray for beauty and popular favor; pray to be charming and witty, give to Queen Venus her own myrtle and mint she loves, and bands of rushes hid in clustered roses" (Ovid *Fasti* 4.135–40). Venus of Eryx was especially honored this day. She had a temple in Rome, but the main temple was at Eryx, on the western tip of Sicily, where sacred prostitution was practiced.

April 25, VI KALENDS MAY

ROBIGA

ROBIGALIA

The festival of Robigalia honored Robiga, the spirit of mildew and rust. This ancient agricultural festival went back into early days of Rome, when the mold-type diseases could destroy an entire crop. Offerings were given to Robiga (the gender of the deity was unclear to Romans) at a sacred grove outside the city walls.

Divinity was perceived, by the Romans, in every act, every moment of the day, down to the smallest needs and mundane tasks of the farmer. There was always a spirit present, whether male or female, god or goddess, often without a name, but with a function to oversee and assure the safety and success of the moment. To worship and honor the spirit that helped a baby take his or her first step unharmed, made sure the candle in the nursery stayed lit, or protected the crops from disease was to experience each moment and each action as sacred.

It is nice to stop during the day at small but special moments, fleeting thoughts, or passing encounters that warm us, like that flash of a smile when our child scores a goal or we feel the sun touching our skin. We should give thanks for the little kindnesses, be grateful for those moments. They can be sacred. The Romans knew the Indigetes, the Invoked Spirits, were present and happy.

The fourth month has passed in which you are honored above all others, Venus. And you know it! (Ovid Fasti 4.13–14)

MAY

THE MONTH
TO BLOSSOM

Use life's flower while it still blooms, for the thorn remains when the roses have fallen away. (Ovid Fasti 5.353–54)

Rural Menologia
SUN IN TAURUS
31 DAYS
NONES: MAY 7
DAYLIGHT: 14 $\frac{1}{2}$ HOURS
DARKNESS: 9 $\frac{1}{2}$ HOURS

Ancient farmers were advised to weed their crops, shear the sheep, wash the wool, break in the young bulls, tend the vegetable garden, and purify the fields. (Menologia)

May bursts on the scene, blossoming forth in an awesome display of pink-, white-, and lavender-shaded flowers. The warm moist air bears traces of a sweet-smelling fragrance, a scent that evokes deeply felt memories and stirs the body and the spirit. A goddess is present, and we know it. May is not a subtle month; new growth surrounds us and cannot be held in check. In the ancient world, spirituality, sexuality, and fertility of earth, animals, and humans were seen as one and honored jointly—especially in May, when flower blossoms first open up with breathtaking beauty. Yet each delicate pink-white flowering blossom on the apple tree portends the luscious ripening summer fruit. Each blossom bears a message to us from the goddess and is a promise of fruition. But Flora can speak for herself.

The Tale of Flora, Goddess of Blossoming Flowers

"Come, Mother of Flowers, and tell us about yourself. Who are you? What are your powers?"

The goddess answered the questions herself, and when she spoke she breathed forth the scent of spring roses. "I am called Flora, yet I was once a nymph of the happy fields. I am too modest to describe my beauty; it was, however, sufficient to win the heart of a god.

One spring day I was roaming the meadows teeming with new green growth and the lush hues of spring's own flowers, when I met the God of Breezes, Zephyr. I became his bride and his wedding gift to me was perpetual spring, the most fertile time of year, when every tree is clothed in green leaves and the ground with grasses and herbs. In the fields that were my dowry lies a fruitful garden cooled by the gentle breeze and watered by a bubbling natural spring.

This garden my husband Zephyr generously filled with blooming flowers of every kind and said to me, "Goddess, be Queen of the Flowers."

So often I have tried to count the colors in the flowerbeds, but could not—there were just too many. At an early hour, as soon as the leaves shake off the morning dew and sunbeams gently warm the blossoms, the Hour Spirits come dressed in colorful clothes to pick my bounteous flowers storing them in light baskets. The Graces assemble in my garden, weaving garlands and wreaths to wear in their hair.

I was the first to scatter new seeds across many foreign lands. Up until then, the earth had been but one dull color. I brought forth the crocus, the narcissus, the hyacinth, the little violets. Perhaps you think that I am only a queen of delicate blossoms, but my divinity and powers influence the tilled fields. If there are many flowers on the stalks of grain, then the threshing floors will be piled high; if the vines have blossomed well, there will be more wine for all; if the olive trees have bloomed in full, then the year will be abundant; if branches of the fruit trees are laden with pink and white blossoms, then the fall harvest will be plentiful. Honey made by the bees is also my gift. I am the goddess who attracts the winged bees to the violet, the clover, and the thyme. I too instill passion in young people, when spirits run high and bodies are lustful.

Before I leave, I have one word of advice. "Use Life's Flower while it still blooms, for the thorn remains when the roses have fallen away."

Flora's tale was ended, and she vanished into thin air. Yet perfumed fragrance lingered. You knew that a goddess had been there.

The flowering month of May is exuberance, innocence, and sexuality all at once. We take in May through our skin's pores, through our senses, and it stirs our sexual longings. In May, we long to be outside baring our bodies to the warm sun, to dig in the earth with our fingers planting seedlings, to gather armfuls of fragrant colorful blossoms, and to fall in love. A beautiful flower stimulates all of our senses with its sweet-smelling fragrance, its rich luxurious color, and its delicate shape. Recall the heady aroma of a lilac in full bloom, or the sight of a velvety rich red rose playing in the sunlight, or a meadow of lilies-of-the-valley blooming in May. Nature's beauty as seen in her blossoms captures the essence of sensuality and sexuality.

In this myth, it is Flora who encourages the flowers to grow and bloom. It is she who bestows magic and allure on the budding blossoms. We are seduced by Flora and her blossoms in May. We are touched by the sensual and sexual qualities inherent in this goddess and her fragrant bounty. Flora teaches us to respond to the natural beauty of May, and not be afraid to use the gift she has given us of life's flower and the essence of our own sexuality. We must learn to celebrate our sensuality and sexuality and glow from within with the same enchantment and beauty possessed by the flower.

May Day festivities observed by many cultures are frivolous and playful rituals, celebrating a time to be sexually alive. To "go Maying" is to venture into the countryside with your lover to gather large bouquets of flowers and gentle the afternoon away. It is nature's way for it is the month of May.

RITES AND RITUALS OF MAY

Macto Esto—*Let It Grow!*

The name for both May and the goddess Maia originated in the Latin root *mag*, or "grow." To fully appreciate May is to recapture the "first blossoming." A young woman "in her May" is first experiencing her sensuality and sexuality. She too is innocent and exuberant as she is coming to love herself and others. A young woman "in her May" glows from within when we behold her.

May 1, Kalends

M A I A

The goddess Maia received sacrifice on the first day of May. This sacrifice of a pregnant sow was the same offering given to Terra Mater, or Mother Earth; hence these two earth goddesses were closely identified.

May 1, KALENDS

BONA DEA

On the first day of May, the temple of Bona Dea, "Good Goddess," was dedicated on the slopes of the Aventine Hill just below a large rock; hence she was officially called Bona Dea at the Rock. Bona Dea was an earth goddess associated with Faunus in myth. Her major ritual was in December.

May 1, KALENDS

LARES PRAESTITES

The Lares Praestites, "Standby Lares," protectors of the state, were honored on May 1. They also had a temple along the Via Sacra, or "Sacred Way," leading through the Forum. The small images of these two gods had worn down with age and apparently a dog sculpted of stone that once stood at their feet had disappeared by Ovid's time.

> A dog fashioned from the same stone used to stand at their feet. What was the reason for its standing with the Lares?
> Both watch over the house, and both are loyal to their master; Lares are night watchmen, and dogs are too. (Ovid *Fasti* 5.135)

We are not so different from the blossoms, you see. We humans can open up when we are touched with sunshine and properly nourished. We anticipate growth and change to come. But it is in May that we feel the first blush—our "coming out." A woman does not have to be young in age to experience May. This blossoming month is a metaphor for growth of any kind at any age. *Macto Esto*, "Let it grow," was an invocation in archaic Latin. It is fitting to invoke the goddess of May. *Macto Esto!*

MODERN RITUAL TO CREATE SACRED SPACE: CULTIVATING FLORA'S GARDEN

There are many books on gardening and a few on sacred space within the garden. One of my favorites is by Elizabeth Murray, *Cultivating Sacred Space: Gardening for the Soul.* In it she says: "When we garden with intent, vision, and a better understanding of how each act in the garden can reflect and enhance our everyday life—then we are creating environments that provide spiritual well-being and nurture for the soul."

Murray echoes the natural cycle of the garden, going season by season reflecting the spiritual qualities of the winter, spring, summer, and fall gardens. Winter she describes as the quiet dormant time of reflection in which will, determination, vision, and a good deal of patience are needed to make it through cold dark months.

Murray shares with us some ancient archetypal symbols that guide us in forming our own sacred landscape. Sacred gardening allows us to wed the wild and the cultivated, to partake in nature's sacred cycle, to tap into our creativity, to root and nurture ourselves. She offers many suggestions for your sacred garden:

- *Altar*—for offerings and ritual
- *Bells*—as an awakening force
- *Bench*—for a contemplative moment
- *Bird feeder*—to invite in the wild birds that were often viewed as epiphanies of the deities
- *Blossoming flowers*—the goddess Flora herself
- *Bridge*—to connect the worlds, with you alone as *pontifex*, or "bridge-builder"
- *Circle*—to recall the natural cycle, with you in the center
- *Color*—for sensual pleasure and to attract Venus and Flora
- *Fountain*—water to recall the essential element of life, the Divine Feminine
- *Garlands*—to honor the deities and ourselves
- *Gateway*—to provide a threshold to cross, and the promise of a new beginning
- *Grotto*—sacred place of the earth goddesses
- *Lantern*—to cast a glow at night
- *Niche*—in a garden wall, a traditional location of a lararium
- *Roses*—for Venus and Isis
- *Statues*—of animals, deities, or figures with special meaning just for you

---

Sacred Scents: The Path to the Deities

May is especially associated with Flora, the Goddess of Blossoming Plants. She is, however, not just a deity of sweet-smelling roses. It is Flora who oversees the tilled fields and blossoming fruit trees. Without Flora, there would be no fruit, no harvest, no honey.

May 3, V NONES

FLORA

FLORALIA

On April 27, the temple of Flora was dedicated, and her games and rituals lasted until May 3. She was a very ancient Goddess of Blossoming Plants. Flora had her own priest and was honored by the oldest college of Roman priests, the Arval Brethren, in their sacred grove.

The games held in honor of Flora at the Circus Maximus included the standard sporting events with two special rites. At some point in the week of festivities, hares and goats, as animals with great fertility and frequent breeding, were released. Also, beans and lupines were scattered in the crowd, again as symbols of fertility and spring. Women were to wear brightly colored clothes, their new spring wardrobes, wear garlands in their hair, entertain at dinners with the tables strewn with roses, and surround themselves with candles and light during the nightly celebrations.

> At parties everyone wears crowns of flowers,
> And the table is strewn with sweet scented roses.
> A guest who drank too much dances with twigs in his hair,
> His indiscretion induced by wine.
> A drunken lover sings loudly at his girlfriend's door,
> With flowers stuck in his hair.
> No serious business is conducted by those who wear flower crowns,
> Nor do they mix water with their wine.
> Bacchus loves flowers and delights in a floral crown...
> Risque shows suit Flora well,
> She is not a goddess of the tragic play.

Her rites are open to all, including prostitutes...
When white robes are worn for Ceres' festival,
Why brightly colored clothes suitable for Flora?
That is because the harvest whitens when the grain is ripe,
But flowers come in a variety of colors.
Flora nodded in agreement.
As she shook her head, flower petals fell from her hair,
As roses strewn on the table. (Ovid *Fasti* 5.338–65)

When we close our eyes and imagine a garden in full bloom with honeysuckle, lilies, oleander, poppies, roses, flowering myrtle, we can understand why the ancient Romans worshiped Flora, Goddess of Blossoms.

Flowers have always been an essential part of any sacred rite. Easter lilies bloom in abundance from the high altars of many Christian churches. Red poinsettias mark the Christmas holidays. Brides take their holy vows wearing flowers in their hair and carrying spectacular sprays of assorted roses, lilies, and baby's breath to celebrate the special day. Flowers are a traditional gift at funerals or to the sick, as they bear a colorful message of hope and renewal. Though garlands of flowers were integral to ancient ritual, sweet-smelling incense and perfumes derived from flowers were equally important. Incense and floral perfume were traditionally used in most ancient rituals, and there were three reasons for this: to mask unpleasant odors, to create a mood, and to delineate a pathway to the gods. In fact, our word "perfume" comes from two Latin words, *per* and *fumus,* and literally means "through the smoke." When either incense or a perfumed object was ignited during a sacred ritual, the fragrant wafts of smoke would spiral high, rising to the heavens and to the very deities themselves. Those sweet smells of perfume and incense carried aloft the prayers and supplications, creating a sacred pathway "through the smoke" to the gods and goddesses. In many ways, May is a gift of nature, a divine gift. It truly is an open doorway to the spirits.

The gods and goddesses are always pleased with a sweet-smelling altar. "Who would bring incense to my burning altars?" questions the god Saturn. Also deities such as Flora made their presence known through scent, for a divine spirit was always associated with a lingering perfumed fragrance. We need to keep this in mind when we lavish floral scent on our body after a bath or dab a drop of exquisite perfume behind our ear as we set out for the day. We are invoking a goddess; we must acknowledge her as part of us.

MODERN RITES OF SPRING WITH PERFUME

Incense and perfume are integral to any ritual. The Roman author Pliny describes the perfume-making process, which involved mixing two main ingredients, the oil and scented substances. He suggests adding a pinch of salt to preserve the oil and a drop of resin to retain the scent, preventing quick evaporation. Oil derived from coarse raw olives was preferred, as it was less greasy, yet almond oil was also used. Roses, lilies, saffron crocus, thyme, and marjoram were among the flowers and herbs commonly used for scent. "Rhodium" was made from rose blossoms, crocus, cinnabar, calamus, and honey. "Oil of Persia," a popular perfume, was a blend of marjoram, lily, fenugreek, myrrh, cassia, cinnamon, myrtle, and laurel. (Donato, 13–15)

Play around with scents this month. Try floral-based bath oils and delve into aromatherapy. Burn scented candles or incense in your home with the windows open so that the perfume rises to the sky and your prayers are carried aloft "through the smoke."

In antiquity, Flora's gift of flowers was vital to ritual. The gods and goddesses were honored with gifts of flowers. In Rome, garlands decorated shops, homes, temples, statues of deities, household altars, and, for certain rites, even farm animals. Worshipers wore wreaths of greens and flowers in their hair. On the Kalends, the Nones, and the Ides of each month, Roman women cleaned their houses in honor of the Hearth Goddess, Vesta. At these times, Cato the Elder recommends decorating the hearth and the home altar with garlands of greens entwined with fragrant blossoms or with bouquets of colorful flowers.

Flowers and garlands were placed or hung at the household shrine. In fact, garland making was a thriving industry at Pompeii. The Roman author Pliny tells a wonderful story to explain how flowers first came to be used. "At first branches of trees or leaves were used; then the custom of using flowers began at Sicyon through the skill of Pausias, the painter, and of the garland-maker Glycera, a lady with whom he was very much in love. When he copied her works in his paintings, to egg him on she varied her designs and there was a duel between Art and Nature" (*Historia Naturalis* 21.4, 23, 27 LCL).

The Romans preferred three kinds of flowers for their garlands: red roses, white lilies, and purple violets. Also for variety they used yellow broom, oleander, bachelor's button, daisies, poppies, amaranth, and cyclamen as well as marigold and assorted wildflowers. Ivy garlands were often entwined with fragrant marjoram, thyme, and mint. Garlands, of course, varied with the seasons, and some flowers were imported from Egypt in winter months. Evergreens and pine were popular in winter as well. Artificial flowers made from dyed flakes of horn were used when fresh were not available. For lasting decoration, pictures of garlands often were painted around the household altar, while hooks were placed in the walls nearby for fresh garlands to be hung.

MODERN RITUAL TO THE BLOSSOMING SEASON: GARLAND MAKING

You too can make a flower wreath with the most exquisite fresh flowers blooming in your garden or available for purchase this month of May. Every May, I gather with my women's group to celebrate this floral season; we always begin in someone's backyard around a picnic table laden with blossoms and herbs. First we wind and twist vines cut from English ivy or wisteria to fit our heads. Then we create our own floral crowns, weaving in brightly colored pansies, pink azaleas, delicate bluish wisteria, and even yellow dandelions. A little mint or rosemary adds a lovely scent as well. Wearing our crowns of flowers, drinking a little wine, eating strawberries, singing songs, reciting poems, laughing, and watching the full moon rise, we know that a goddess must be close by.

You can also make a garland to hang around your neck or add beauty and fragrance to your home. In May, I always recall my mother telling how she and her friends picked armfuls of daisies and strung them together to form one long daisy chain that was draped over the shoulders of the women graduating from the small college in Virginia. The ancient garland is similar to a Hawaiian lei. You make one by selecting a long thin needle (they sell special ones just for lei making) and thread. Then, sew the blossoms together. It is wise to sprinkle the flowers with water to keep them fresh as you work. You might place the completed garland in the refrigerator until use.

Be Cautious, Beware, and Begone!

As Roman farmers knew, a cautious time soon followed quickly on the heels of frivolity. Mid-May was the time when hungry ghosts walked the earth. Protection was essential for oneself and the lives of one's family, because these ghosts came right into the home! After the Ides, it was time to purify the fields and protect the baby animals and new, tender seedlings. The "lemures" and other night-stalking evil spirits had to be chased away to ensure survival of the newly blossoming growth. May is a time to rejoice in the sensual beauty all around, yet BEWARE! May is a two-edged sword. You must always be on guard and watch your back, as the Romans did literally in the festival of Lemuria, held in mid-May.

May 9, 11, 13; VII, V, III IDES

LEMURIA

According to the ancient rite, the head of the family got up at midnight with bare feet, avoiding using any type of knots in clothing or sandals. He made a protective gesture with the hand where the thumb is held between closed fingers. He then washed his hands in pure water and walked through the house spitting black beans out his mouth, repeating the prayer, "With these beans I redeem me and mine." This prayer had to be repeated nine times without looking backward and with face averted. The ghosts then came and picked up the beans in compensation for the living souls. The master washed his hands and, using bronze instruments, made a loud clashing noise. Then he repeated nine times the chant, "Ghosts of my Fathers and Ancestors, be gone!" He could then look backward throughout the house and the ghosts would be placated and gone (Ovid *Fasti* 5.438–44).

The *lemures* were hungry spirits of the dead who return to stalk the living kin. These night-stalkers were terrifying spirits, not the "friendly dead" we met in February. These potentially harmful spirits walked the earth in early May and could enter the home. The evil spirits were hailed as the wandering and terrifying ghosts of men and women who had died untimely deaths. The use of bronze instruments in this magical rite harkens to a prehistoric period. In fact, the rite was so old, Ovid and other Romans did not fully understand its origin, even though they most likely got up at midnight and conducted the litany. Appeasement of evil spirits stalking the household was essential for growth of new life.

The Romans viewed May as a time when the veil between the two worlds of the very alive and the very dead was thin. To the Romans, May was like November, the opposing month on the calendar when the shades of the underworld and ghosts of the dead mingled with the living. The Lemuria was celebrated on three nonconsecutive days, usually the seventh, fifth, and third days before the full moon of May. This rite was similar to February's purification rites, but much more fearful.

May 11, V IDES

MANIA

Mania was the mother of the Lares, and though her name means "good one," she is a death goddess. When a family was threatened with harm or in danger, an effigy or doll resembling Mania was hung on the front door. Cakes of flour in the shape of ugly human figures were offered.

May 14, I IDES

THE ARGEI

After a preliminary sacrifice, the priests and Vestal Virgins together with other citizens threw from a sacred bridge over the Tiber River thirty effigies made to look like men and called Argei. The priestess, the *flaminica* who accompanied the procession, was forbidden to comb her hair that day and she had to display signs of mourning. The Argei puppets were apparently made of rushes. The ritual was a great act of purification from evils accumulated during the year as the Argei were the personifications of the demons.

Just as new green seedlings push through the soil shooting to the sun on thin stalks or the soft downy ducklings venture from their mothers, we too can be vulnerable at this time of birth and early growth. May is a time to be merry, yet not reckless. May was an unlucky time for marriages and we are told that only "bad women" married in May.

We also know that caution is most appropriate during such an exuberant period of early growth. The young are fragile, innocent, and unknowing. The young girl "in her May" needs advice from an older and wiser voice. The ingenue requires protection from mean-spirited people who can cause great harm or who carry the touch of death. We too can do harm to ourselves from lack of experience. The ancient Romans understood this and saw the need to protect themselves and their households with ritual. Awareness of the dangers and wise decisions at this juncture can prevent harm, ensure continual growth through the summer months, and guarantee fruition.

MODERN BANISHING RITUAL

Don't get carried away in the exuberance of May. This can be a difficult month when you might have to face some unpleasant things. May can be a month when troubles and problems arise, a time when the "dark shades" are trying their best to pull you down. In fact, they may even enter you house and sanctuary and touch you "close to home." As you indulge your senses in all the wonderful blossoming days of May, watch carefully for the dark side.

In the most ancient tradition of the Argei, fashion your own puppet or doll of rushes, reeds, or twigs. After investing this doll with all of your fears, problems, or concerns, discard the doll. The Roman Vestal Virgins threw their Argei into the Tiber; you also could heave it into a flowing stream or river and watch those cares just float away.

Good Fortune and Fertility

May ends with rituals for *bona fortuna,* good fortune and fertility. The favor of the fertility goddess Dea Dia was sought through the intercession of her priests, the Arval Brethren, or Field Brothers.

May 25, VIII KALENDS JUNE

FORTUNA PRIMIGENIA

Fortuna Primigenia, also called Fortuna Publica, was honored during this last week of the month. She was an ancient Italic goddess, the Bringer of Increase. She was also associated with Tyche, or "Luck." At her oracle and large temple at Praeneste, inscribed tablets of oak were drawn from a chest at random. The worshipers had to interpret the message for themselves.

May 29, IV KALENDS JUNE

DEA DIA

The goddess Dea Dia was worshiped by the group of priests called the Arval Brethren, or "Field Brothers," on this day in May. Her name and origin are quite old and little is known of her. Her name is possibly associated with the increasing sunlight, yet certainly with fertility and agricultural prosperity. Their sacred grove was located about five miles outside Rome, near the modern site of La Magliana. There were twelve members of the collegium, chosen from the senatorial families; the emperor was always a member. The group of priests selected from among themselves every year a president, or *magister,* and a head priest, or *flamen.*

Their main function was to conduct the ritual to Dea Dia on May 29, but they also celebrated the emperor's birthday and other special events. The sacred grove has been partially excavated, and it contained a temple to Dea Dia, a dining hall, a bathing complex, and other cult buildings. During the ritual to Dea Dia, the brotherhood of priests gathered at her temple in the grove and sang a prayer to invoke Mars and other spirits.

The Ambarvalia was likewise a lustration or purification of the land. "We purify the crops and fields in the fashion handed down from our ancestors of old" (Tibullus 2.1). The type of sacrifice was a *suovetaurilia*, which literally means in Latin "pig, sheep, and bull." The three animals were led around the fields three times and then offered to Mavors, Father Mars, the ancient Roman agricultural god, and to Dea Dia, Goddess of Vegetation and Growth.

May 27–29, MOVEABLE RITUAL FROM VI–IV KALENDS JUNE

AMBARVALIA

The Ambarvalia, or the "Beating of the Bounds," was a festival held during the last weeks of May. The fields of the farmer were purified from evil influences just as the houses were in the Lemuria. A magic circle was created by a procession around the fields or the sacred space in need of purification, while offerings were made to the appropriate deities. A town could be purified as well during the Ambarvalia by a similar process of lustration.

In addition to Mars, the agricultural deities Ceres and Bacchus were invoked at this time to promote growth. On this holy day, men, women, and animals had to rest. The farmer put garlands around his oxen's horns. Women lay aside their spinning, and all celebrants had to be ritually clean with hands washed in a ceremony. No sexual intercourse during the prior night was allowed. Virgil tells us that at the Ambarvalia, the procession with crowns of oak leaves went around the fields three times, singing and dancing, urging Ceres to come to their homes (*Georgics* 1.345).

The end of May has come. "I pray to you, Flora, Goddess shower me with your gifts." (Ovid Fasti 5.379)

JUNE
THE MONTH
TO NURTURE

There is a sacred grove dense with trees, a place
Shut off from all noise except the roar of a waterfall.
Here I came to meditate quietly, to question the origin of this month just begun.
I was just pondering this month's name.
Blessed Be! I saw goddesses, . . .
I trembled; the pallor of my face belied my awestruck feeling.
Then, the awesome goddess herself, comforted me by saying,
So you will not remain ignorant, nor make a mistake,
The month of June gets its name from me . . .
You will now read of Juno's month. (Ovid Fasti 6.3–26 passim, 63)

Rural Menologia
SUN IN GEMINI
30 DAYS
NONES: JUNE 5
DAYLIGHT: 15 HOURS
DARKNESS: 9 HOURS
SOLSTICE

⤛⤜•⤙⤚

Ancient farmers were advised to mow and cut the hay and loosen the soil around the grapevines. (Menologia)

Relax and take a deep breath—June has arrived. This is the month to settle in with a greater sense of comfort and security. The sun shines on the longest day of the year, giving the gift of life and growth. Crops are ripening. May's blossoms are now transformed into tiny green apples on the tree—not yet ripe and ready for picking, but safely on their way. All is more restful now than in May. June is not a time for playful sexuality, but instead a time for slow and steady growth.

The month of June settles in the same way a new mother settles down to nurse her baby, with fullness, gentle strokes, and loving glances. The mother settles down to caress her precious newborn offering, her breast teeming with warm mother's milk. The mother sits and calmly nurses, her power is "standing by" power; she is all-enduring. The month of June begins in the same nurturing way with a sense of warm fullness. Now, there is no fear of cold nights. All things grow and are abundant.

We bid welcome to June with a sigh of accomplishment, the same long, deep groan we uttered as we gave the final push and birthed our babies. That is a primordial sigh, one that comes from deep, deep down. A job well done! It is the same contented feeling we enjoy when we bring anything deeply meaningful to fruition, whether it is birthing a child, completing a project, preparing a special meal, or watching the garden we labored hours over bloom. We have all experienced that moment of complete satisfaction at some point in our lives. June is the month Mother Earth sighs! And we each can feel it.

This is a very stable month, a month to take root, turn toward the warm sun and grow. We have passed through the months of introspection, planning, and exuberance. Now is the time to get down to business, and nature's business is to grow and flourish. June is the month of the mother and young baby, the Queen of Heaven and her Child. This is the time to honor that divine and natural bond. The natural world, mothering, and the sacred are so intimately entwined, as you read in the myth of Juno and the birth of Mars. June is Mother Juno's month, fittingly named after her.

Juno and the Birth of Mars

When the goddess Minerva was born, motherless and fully clothed, from the head of Jupiter, awesome Juno, his wife, was angered that her services were not required. On her way to visit Ocean to complain of her husband's deed, Juno grew both tired and hungry. She stopped at the door of Flora, the Goddess of Blooming Flowers.

"What brings you to my home, O Divine Juno, daughter of the great Saturn?" questioned Flora as she received the Queen of Heaven.

Juno began to describe her journey and her husband Jupiter's great insult, as sweet-smelling Flora tried her best to console her friend with kind words. "My distress cannot be healed with gentle words, dear Flora," said the great goddess. "Jupiter became a father and gave birth to a daughter on his own. He did this without lying with me or any woman. The child has no mother. Jupiter, instead, serves as both father and mother, uniting both roles unto himself. So why, O Flora, should I relinquish the hope of becoming a mother without a man, a husband? This can be done. I need no man. I will remain chaste, untouched by man and yet give birth. I will try all the drugs and herbs in the wide world, and I will explore the deep seas and the depths of Hell for a way."

Juno's speech would have flowed on, had she not noticed a look of uncertainty on Flora's face.

"Flora, my nymphlike friend, it seems that you may have some power to help me in my cause? I know that you fear my husband Jupiter's wrath if he should ever find out, yet I promise that your name will always be kept a secret. I swear by the waters of Hell, that Jupiter will never know."

"Then, your wish of a chaste and virginal birth can be accomplished," confided the Flower Goddess, "with the use of this rare and unique flower sent to me from the fields of Olenus. It is the only flower of its type in my garden. The one who gave it to me advised me of its use in making a barren heifer pregnant. It is accomplished with only a touch of the flower's petals."

At once, Flora pinched off the clinging flower with her thumb and held it to Juno's breast. The great goddess Juno conceived at once as the flower gently touched her bosom. And now, pregnant with child, Juno's wish was granted. She became a mother without the touch of a man. She was delivered of her holy child, and thus the awesome god Mars was born.

This myth has come to us from most ancient prehistoric times, for it is a story of the Great Goddess. She is all-powerful as life-giver and nurturer. Here Juno, queen of the gods and goddesses, is Creatrix and Mother. And she neither wants nor needs a man. Juno does not shy away from direct confrontation with her husband, Jupiter. On the contrary, when ignored by her husband, she does not meekly submit to his display of power or lash out indiscriminately. She instead sets out to establish her own position independent of Jupiter. Juno is very clever, for she knows where her ultimate source of power resides—and that is in the natural world. It lies with the perennial flower that grows every spring. Fertility, potency, and the abundance essential for the continuity of all life reside within nature and the female. The great goddess Juno is Mother Earth, impregnated by the earth's own seed—the flower. She is female fertility and potency incarnate. Juno is the ultimate Mother, and June is her month!

We too can look to Juno as a source of feminine energy and power, and what a wonderful role model to select. Juno is a not a simple deity; on the contrary, she is a complex goddess as she alone fulfills the many and diverse female roles of Creatrix, Protectress, Warner, Nurturer, and Mother. In this myth, she proves herself the equal to Jupiter by establishing a magical, sacred bond with the natural world and creation. Her actions are direct, deliberate, and clever, for Juno is a very determined goddess who will succeed in her quest. Juno is the potential of all women manifest in one great goddess.

As women, we each possess Juno's feminine energy when we are expected to perform similar duties in our daily lives, caring for ourselves and our families, establishing our power in a male world, nurturing, protecting, and mothering our ideas, ourselves, and our children to fruition. The strength and potential of this goddess resides within each of us.

RITES AND RITUALS OF JUNE

Protecting from Harm

Capture for a moment those maternal feelings and sensations. More than anything, the mother wants her baby to be healthy, to be safe, to be happy, to grow. The young babe finds safety and comfort enfolded in the mother's strong arms, seeking the warm milk and the intimate bond of mother and child. June is the month to get in touch with those feelings and seize them for ourselves. This month the lessons from nature involve nurturing, mothering, safety, and security. Energy this month is not channeled into sexual arousal, but into nurturing, protecting, and caregiving. The goddesses honored this month were strong defenders of family and home, Juno the Warner, Mother Matuta, and Vesta the Hearth Keeper. We too can feel safe in the care of these great goddesses.

Juno the Warner keeps lookout and warns us if trouble is coming. Mother Juno protects the fledgling. If we really want to feel safe, we need to look to Juno. Juno Moneta, Juno the "Warner," will send a message if harm is coming. She did so for the Romans when they were under attack. We must be sure to listen to our inner voice for her subtle messages and pay heed to her stern words of warning. When there is new growth, we especially must honor Juno Moneta.

June 1, KALENDS

JUNO MONETA

The Kalends of every month were sacred to the goddess Juno. And in this lunar capacity, she was a true moon goddess. It was Juno who oversaw a woman's menstrual cycle, helping to regulate and ease the pain of monthly periods. In the earliest times, after the sighting of the slender crescent moon each month, the high priest and priestess sacrificed to Juno. On the Kalends of June, the goddess was especially honored as Juno Moneta, or "Juno the Warner."

Too often we ignore our inner voice, our intuition saying "Slow down," "Think this over," "This path is wrong, don't take it." But we must listen! This is the voice of the "Warner"; she resides inside each of us. Her voice may be faint and her message subtle, but it is nonetheless genuine. She is a very valuable goddess and one not to trifle with or ignore. We too can hear her call and heed her warnings if only we are attentive and give credence to those self-doubts and moments of hesitation that we feel on occasion. We must come to view our intuitive side as a gift of the goddess Juno. Her warnings saved many a Roman life and may prove to be a valuable ally.

Our word "money" comes from the name Juno Moneta in a roundabout fashion. The temple of Juno Moneta was dedicated on June 1, 344 B.C.E., and stood on top of the Capitoline Hill. The title of Moneta, or "Warner," was given in antiquity to Juno because she, through the intercession of her sacred geese, warned the Romans of an attack by the Gauls. It was also said that during an earthquake a voice came from Juno's temple instructing the people to offer sacrifice. Because the Romans built the state mint for striking official coins adjacent to Juno Moneta's temple, the goddess became associated with the minting of coins. "Moneta" came to be synonymous with coins, and the origin for our word "money."

In modern times, June is a special month for brides and the season for weddings. Juno's name may have originated in the word for "bride" or "young woman" (juvenis), because Juno was the consummate bride of Jupiter. Ironically, the first weeks of June in the ancient calendar were considered unfavorable for weddings. Marriages were to be avoided before the full moon, as this was considered a dangerous time when harmful spirits walked the earth—a time to be careful. The full moon brought good fortune to women. "Don't make any big plans before midmonth and do not get married," advised the ancient priestess.

> I have a daughter and I pray she lives longer than I.
> If she is safe and well, I will always be happy.
> When I wished to give her in marriage,
> I asked what days were lucky for the wedding and which were not.
> I learned that June only after the sacred Ides is good for brides and grooms.
>   (Ovid, Fasti 6.219–25)

MODERN RITUAL TO HONOR
JUNO AND WOMEN

On the Kalends, Ides, and Nones, Roman women tending the home had the task of cleansing the hearth and making it pure. Following the lunar cycle, the home and hearth were scrubbed clean. Fresh flowers and newly made garlands were placed around the home and central hearth. Nothing extravagant was needed for Juno. It is important for us all to respect the home, and women's work in the home, because this is sacred work for renewal of the inner spirit.

Keep a fresh bouquet of flowers in a special vase in your kitchen where you can see and enjoy them as you prepare meals and wash dishes. Light some candles in the kitchen as you work.

Protecting Family and Health

Carna was an ancient goddess with a temple on the Caelian Hill. According to myth, Carna was given special powers to ward off evil vampires or bloodsuckers, called *striges*. These were terrifying nocturnal birds who preyed on young babies in the nursery at night.

> *They have large heads, bulging eyes, beaks suited for tearing flesh,*
> *Grayish feathers and hooked claws.*
> *At night, they fly into the nursery seeking young children who still nurse at*
> *the breast.*
> *They mutilate the bodies, snatching them from the cradles.*
> *It is said that they tear the flesh of babes not yet weaned*
> *And drink the blood until their bellies are full. (Ovid Fasti 6.133–38)*

June 1, KALENDS

C A R N A

C A R N E R I A

The Kalends of June were popularly known as the Bean Kalends, because beans were given as an offering to this goddess.

> "Why is a meal of fatty bacon and beans with barley served
> On the Kalends of this month?" you ask.
> Carna is a goddess from the oldest times. She lives on simpler foods.
> And does not partake in luxurious banquets.
> Back then, the fish swam safely, not caught and eaten by the people.
> Oysters were safe in their shells.
> The peacock pleased human taste only by its colorful feathers.
> In those olden days, Earth did not send wild animals out to be hunted down,
> The pig was prized and provided meat for special occasions.
> From the soil, grew only beans and hardy barley.
> Whoever eats a combination of these two foods on the Kalends of the sixth month
> Will have a healthy digestive system, or so they say.
>
> (Ovid *Fasti* 6.170–81)

As a protectress, Carna was also the Goddess of Internal Organs. The Romans prayed for health. She highly recommends bean meal and bacon fat. Carna is the vegetarian's patroness, for meat was not part of her usual diet.

~~~~~~

MODERN RITUAL FOR GOOD HEALTH

Carna watches over your diet very carefully. She herself delights in the simplest foods, those that can easily be grown in rich soil such as beans and barley. Pork was only eaten on very special occasions. Honor Carna by establishing a healthy diet.

An ancient recipe using fava beans for good digestion and a healthy body comes from the Roman chef Apicius: "Serve the beans with ground mustard, honey, pine nuts, rue, cumin and vinegar" (Apicius 5.6.3). Here is a modern version. You may wish to make a smaller amount.

FABACIAE, OR FAVA BEAN SALAD *(serves 6)*

2 pounds fresh fava beans
$^1/_2$ teaspoon dried mustard
I teaspoon honey

$^1/_2$ teaspoon cumin
vinegar, to taste

Shell beans and boil in salted water. Make the dressing: mix the mustard with honey and dilute with vinegar. Pour the dressing over the beans, sprinkle with cumin, and serve.

Keeping the Hearth

Come, Vesta,
To live in this beautiful home.
Come with warm feelings of friendship.
Bring your intelligence,
Your energy and your passion
To join with your goodwill.
Burn brightly at my hearth.
Burn always in my soul.
You are welcome here.
I remember you. (Homeric Hymn)

Vesta was the Roman Hearth Goddess, whose worship surely went far back into prehistoric times, when each family honored the spirit of the hearth fire burning in the center of their round thatched hut. The first altar was the circular hearth of the ancient round hut. Family and guests who sat around the burning hearth fire and gazed into the sacred flame felt the warmth and nurturing. They understood this as sacred space.

June 7, VII IDES

TEMPLE OF VESTA OPENED

June 7 was the first day of an eight-day ritual to Vesta held every year. During this period the round temple of Vesta in the Roman Forum and the inner sanctum, which was called the *penus*, or storehouse, was opened to the female public— only women were allowed to enter. The women, it seems, had to enter the temple barefoot to honor the goddess.

As Vesta is the Living Flame, she is especially important for her part in ritual: "Vesta is crucial for conducting ritual. No sacrifice or ritual can be conducted without fire. She must first be invoked at all ritual" (Servius *Aeneid* 1.292). The kindling of the hearth fire or the lighting of a candle before a ritual assures her presence.

All rituals were begun by the lighting of a sacrificial flame on the altar. Hence, Vesta as the Living Flame was invoked at all rites with a short prayer to welcome her. In olden days, it was the custom to sit around the hearth fire in the center of the modest thatched hut. The gods were invited to join at the meal while a clean platter was heaped with food offered to Vesta.

In each home, devout Romans would offer a prayer and sacrifice every day to Vesta at the household altar, the *lararium*. The mother or father would lead a short service to pray for the family's prosperity, a warm and welcoming hearth, and a fully stocked pantry.

Vesta provides sacred space for the family to gather, where outsiders and guests are welcomed. Feeling close to the spirit of Vesta is feeling the warmth and safety of the home. Vesta provides a place of harmony and a place to gather. We can usually tell a home in which Vesta is honored because we feel welcome. We can create such a home for ourselves by asking Vesta in as the ancients did.

We entreat her presence by lighting candles or kindling a fire in the hearth. Vesta needs no statuettes; in fact there are very few images of her from antiquity. "Conceive of Vesta as nothing but the living flame . . . *vivam flammam*" (Ovid *Fasti* 6.295–98, 291).

The Latin word for hearth is *focus,* which is derived from older words meaning "to be bright" and "to strengthen." To be in focus was to place an offering on the hearth, or *in foco.* Vesta is the "mistress of the hearths" (*Vesta domina focorum*). It is she who urges us to be quiet, to sit, to gaze, to listen, and to use all of our senses including intuition. It is she who gives us sacred space and quiet time to regain our inner power—female power. *Vi stando,* or standing-by power, is the power of Vesta and her gift to us. "Vesta is the same as the earth. . . . The earth stands by its own power; Vesta's power is called standing-by power" or "*Stat vi terra sua: vi stando Vesta vocatur*" (Ovid *Fasti* 6.298–99).

The Hearth Goddess is likewise a tribute to the importance of the home—a safe, secure place and a sanctuary we return to daily. The ancient people spoke of their Hearth Goddess as a "stay-at-home." She was unable to join in the processions of the gods or frolic with the other deities in secluded groves on Mt. Olympus. Why? Because the hearth was fixed in the center of the home and could not be moved—neither could the goddess. She is home-based. This is good—"at-homeness." This is a time to sit quietly around the sacred hearth, to weave, to cook, to nurse a baby, to create, to be with oneself. This is a time for introspection and a time to gather one's thoughts and energies.

June 7–13, VII IDES TO IDES

VESTA

VESTALIA

These eight days in June were specially honored by the bakers and millers. Fornax, the Oven Goddess, has her own rites in February, but in the oldest times, bread was baked in the hearth fire—Vesta's domain. The bread was buried in the hot ashes and a broken piece of tile placed on top. For this reason Vesta became the patroness of the bakers and millers. Garlands were hung from the necks of the donkeys used to turn the mills, offerings were made to Vesta of sacred cakes, and a feast was enjoyed by all worshipers.

June 15, XVI Kalends July

TEMPLE OF VESTA CLOSED

The day was called *Quando stercum delatum fas,* because the filth was swept from the temple of Vesta on this day. The temple was then closed to the public, and business would resume after the sweeping. The filth was taken down an alley beside the Capitoline Hill and carried to the Tiber River, where it was thrown in. This marked the official purification of the temple of Vesta and the public hearth.

Focus is a gift of Vesta. Focus is a very important need for women who spend much of their time rushing around with work and family. We can easily lose focus, which also means we lose energy. At times, we might use such phrases to describe ourselves as feeling "off base," "off center," "spaced out," or "off the wall." These words all describe space and the lack of centering. We have lost touch with Vesta. When we have lost focus, the wrong thing to do is to rush around trying to gain it back. To regain focus, we must sit quietly and center ourselves at the sacred hearth fire. We need a quiet time and a solitary time for ourselves in a warm nurturing place.

It was fire at the hearth that could shine a light into the terrifying darkness, blanket the home in warmth from a bitter cold night, and transform raw dough into delicious smelling, life-sustaining bread. Transformation and renewal are also gifts of Vesta. The hearth fire has long been associated with renewal and rejuvenation. We have experienced the restorative qualities of sitting quietly before the hearth fire. After rushing through a mad day at the workplace or with childcare we need to cleanse, heal, and purify ourselves in the shelter of a warm, nurturing, Vesta-loved home. Keeping the hearth or the home space pure and not polluted by work and public life is essential.

MODERN RITUAL AND MEDITATION TO THE HEARTH GODDESS

PRAYER TO VESTA

Vesta,
You who take care of the sacred hearth,
Come into this house of mine,
Come on in here.
Be gracious toward my prayer.

Welcome Vesta and regain your inner power, your *vi stando*, your standing-by power. Allow Vesta to nurture you with a spark of light.

Since the goddess Vesta is the "Living Flame," you too can invoke her when you wish. Simply strike a match and light a fire. Here is a wonderful candle gazing exercise from Starhawk:

In a quiet, darkened room, light a candle. Ground and center, and gaze quietly at the candle. Breathe deeply, and let yourself feel warmed by the light of the candle. Let its peaceful radiance fill you completely. As thoughts surface in your mind, experience them as if they came from outside. Do not let the flame split into a double image; keep your eyes focused. Remain for at least five to ten minutes and then relax." (*Spiral Dance* 65–66)

Nurturing Growth

The Matralia was held on June 11, or three days before the full moon, to honor the goddess Mater Matuta, worshiped throughout Italy. She was the Goddess of Motherhood and Growth. In Ovid's day, women prayed not for their own children, but for those of their sisters on June 11. There is some confusion, however, because in the oldest times the word for sister, *soror,* is similar to *soriare,* which means "the growth of female breasts." It seems more appropriate that a good mother would pray to Mater Matuta to take care of her adolescent daughter on this day and ensure her growth into a woman. Ovid tells the story of how Matuta, after wandering with her son, came to be honored by the Roman people.

June 11, III IDES

M A T E R   M A T U T A

M A T R A L I A

The rites to Mother, or Mater Matuta, in Rome were somewhat unusual. On this day, her cult statue was decorated and adorned with garlands and gifts only by women who had been married one time. Female slaves were forbidden inside the temple this day, although one was selected to be ritually slapped on the head. Sacred cakes of libum were offered to the goddess Mater Matuta. They were cooked by the old method in earthen pots.

> You, Mater Matuta, say that you entered the home of faithful Carmenta as
>   a guest
> And after a long period of starvation, you satisfied your hungry cravings.
> Carmenta immediately prepared the cakes herself,
> And quickly put them on the hearth to bake.
> Even to this day, Matuta loves baked cakes at her festival, the Matralia,
> This kindly gesture is more welcome to the goddess than more expensive
>   offerings.
> "Now, O Prophetess, tell me what lies in my future, as much as you may
> I pray to you that you include this request with your hospitality."

She [Carmenta] paused a few moments.
Then, a holy spirit entered the prophetess and she was filled with divinity.
You would scarcely have recognized the prophetess Carmenta
For she appeared at once so much holier, so much grander.
"Rejoice, your suffering is over, Ino [Matuta]," she said.
"You will always prosper among these people [the Romans]. . . .
You will be called *matuta* by our people,
Your son will rule over harbors, we will call him Portunus.
Matuta nodded and pledged fidelity.
She and her son ended their wanderings and changed their names.
He is a god, she is a goddess. (Ovid *Fasti* 6.528–50 passim)

The goddess had a famous temple at Satricum, where offerings to her that have come to light include clay models of inner organs, figurines of swaddled babies, and statues of mothers holding children. All these artifacts confirm Mater Matuta's reign over the mother and child relationship, nurturing, and growth.

A shrine to Mater Matuta also stood near the modern town of Capua where a collection of magnificent statues, life size or slightly smaller, can be found in the museum. The statues dedicated to Mater Matuta are of seated women, ample mothers holding swaddled babies in their arms. One silent mother holds twelve infants, six in each arm. It is thought that the statues, dedicated by local women, lined a pathway to the temple of Mater Matuta as though they were a row of eternally protective nurturing mothers.

MODERN RITUAL TO NURTURE
AND MOTHER YOURSELF

"I remember when I was a little girl," Helen began, "when the sky turned dark with thick black clouds, and the wind howled around the house, lightning flashed sharply cutting a jagged path in the sky, thunder boomed so loud it shook the house, and the rain pelted down on the roof. Mother would find me and scoop me up in her warm safe arms. She sat me before the large picture window and wrapped me up in a warm, soft blanket from head to toe. Here we would sit together watching the storm and drinking hot cocoa. This is one of my favorite memories."

When uncertain or fearful times arise, we each crave to be mothered and loved, to feel safe and know that all will turn out fine. In truth, we secretly want to be swaddled in a warm blanket, fed a richly satisfying hot drink, and be held—just held.

By chance a fierce storm unleashed its full fury during a gathering of my women's group one summer's eve. As Helen shared her memory of storms and mothering, each grown woman slowly reached for a blanket or throw. We swaddled ourselves, drank tea, and watched the storm pass while sharing fearful thoughts or memories mingled with sympathetic comments and gentle hugs. What was truly apparent was how much each of us desperately needed mothering—something we do for others, but never for ourselves. It was a gentle, healing evening and we felt better for it. Mothering qualities are essential for growth. Spend some time learning how to best mother yourself.

Soulful Music

June was the time when the flute players, or *tibicines*, honored Minerva. It was the *tibicines* who played sacred music for all rituals and sacrifices held in Rome. Apparently, the Roman officials in 311 B.C.E. forbade the *tibicines* from holding their annual banquet. The flute players held a strike, refused to play at any religious ritual, and withdrew to the town of Tivoli.

When the Senate gave in and asked the *tibicines* to return so that the rites could continue, they promised the sacred musicians they could "for three days a year roam through the city in festive robes, making music and enjoying the license that is now customary, and to those who played at religious ceremonies the right of dining at the temple"(Livy 9.30). It seems that on June 13–15, the flute players would roam the streets of Rome, wearing masks and the long robes of women, and play music "in the midst of serious business, both public and private" (Valerius Maximus 2.5.6).

June 13–15, IDES TO XVI KALENDS JULY

JUPITER AND MINERVA

LESSER QUINQUATRUS

The Greater Quinquatrus to Minerva was celebrated on March 19–23, and the lesser rites to Minerva were held on June 13–15. Minerva, as the Goddess of Flutes and Pipes, explains:

> "My festival called the Quinquatrus is celebrated in March," Minerva said.
> "I am the Patroness of Flute Players!
> I was the first to make the long flute pipes
> Resonate with music by cutting holes at intervals in boxwood.
> It pleased me to play the flute.
> But when I saw my face reflected in a pool of clear water,
> My youthful cheeks were all puffed out.
> The sound of the flute is not worth that,
> Good-bye, dear flute, I said. . . .
> Nevertheless, I am the inventor of the flute and the first composer of
>   flute music.
> That is why this day is sacred to flute players." (Ovid *Fasti* 6.695–710)

Music has always played a vital role in ritual. Hymns or paeans were commonly sung to Apollo, Bacchus, and Aesculapius. Singing of hymns, such as the "Hymn to Mars" and the "Hymn of the Arval Brethren," traditionally accompanied a formal act of worship. Instrumental music was integral to Roman worship, and if a pipe player suddenly became silent, the ritual was tainted. Possibly the sound of the music was thought to drown out ill omens and keep harmful spirits from the sacred rites. The type of music may not have mattered, for the Romans did not prohibit the introduction of new forms for their ritual acts. There are a few surviving scores, and modern musicians have even recreated and recorded some ancient Roman music. Horace wrote a fine tribute to Augustus's New Age ceremony in 17 B.C.E. sung by a chorus of twenty-seven young voices. In the fall, Ceres delights in a new song made up just for her harvest.

Good Fortune!

Fors was the ancient Goddess of Fate and Luck, and Fortuna, the Goddess of Good Luck and Fortune, as her name implies. At some early date, these two Roman deities were worshiped as one, Fors Fortuna. She is honored at midsummer with raucous parties and celebrations.

June 24, VII KALENDS JULY

FORS FORTUNA

Time is slipping away, and we grow old as the years quietly glide by.
The unbridled days pass by one by one.
Already the day for honoring the goddess Fors Fortuna has arrived.
Just seven more days and June will be over.
Come citizens of Rome, celebrate the goddess Fors Fortuna with great joy.
Her temple along the Tiber River was a gift from a king.
Hurry those of you coming by foot or those riding in a swift boat.
It is no shame to return home from her rites slightly inebriated.
The boats decorated with garlands carry parties of youthful revelers.
A lot of wine is consumed in the middle of the river.
The people worship this goddess
Since King Servius who built her temple began life as a commoner.
Slaves worship this goddess
Since the mother of King Servius was a slave. (Ovid *Fasti* 6.771–82)

June 24 must have been a day of boating parties and celebrations accompanied by many cups of wine. Cicero asks, "Whoever experienced so much delight from sailing down the Tiber on the day of the festival [to Fors Fortuna]?" (*De Finibus Bonorum et Malorum* 5.70).

June is now over. "All honor comes with the month's name... This is truly the month of Juno." (Ovid Fasti 6.76)

JULY

THE MONTH
TO SAVOR

Honor Adonis with all things beautiful. Beside him lie all ripe fruits that the tall trees bear. (Theocritus, Hymn to Adonis)

Rural Menologia
SUN IN CANCER
31 DAYS
NONES: JULY 7
DAYLIGHT: $14^{1}/_{2}$ HOURS
DARKNESS: $9^{3}/4$ HOURS

Ancient farmers were advised to harvest the beans and the barley. They were to gather in and harvest the ripened fruits of the earth. (Menologia)

⁂

July is a month of fruition. Nature's bounty is ripe, plump, and ready to be picked. All the planning of January, the intense preparation of February, the exciting and sexual months of April and May, and the quieter nurturing days of June have brought us to July. The fruit we tended is now fully ripe and ready for picking. Allow yourself to feel the fullness, the ripeness. Seek out some shade and walk through the old grove of lemon trees with bright yellow fruit giving off an intoxicating citrus scent. In an orchard grab down a peach from a low hanging branch and sink your teeth into it, letting the sweet juices dribble into your mouth. Taste the deep purple grapes bursting with pulp and promise of a good vintage. Apples and cherries and luscious berries are reaching a point of full, round ripeness. The sun has been good to them. Our crops have been nurtured into full growth. July begins the harvest, when the fully ripe fruit is picked.

The cycle of nature must continue—there is no other way. This is at no time more apparent than in July—a critical turning point in the agricultural year. July marks a transition from growth to death, sunlight to darkness, joy to sadness. It is a month to experience highs then lows, gain then loss. There is, however, as the Adonis myth foretells, always the promise of another growing season, a new spring, and a rebirth.

Adonis, whose name means simply "Lord," was a most beautiful young man born from an incestuous union. His mother, Myrrha, pregnant by her own father, was transformed into a tree, the weeping myrrh. Nine months later Adonis emerged from the tree, as the myth relates. Aphrodite fell in love with the handsome youth and entrusted him to Persephone, who refused to return him. Zeus resolved the conflict by announcing that Adonis would live four months with Persephone, four with Aphrodite, and four with his own choice. He was later killed while hunting and his blood stains the anemone; that of Aphrodite running to his aid stains the red rose.

Now read of his death in the fullness of his life. In the myth, Adonis was sacrificed, as he had to be, for out of his dead body grew the small red anemone. Adonis, God of All Growing and Dying Life, God of Vegetation, had to die to be reborn.

The Death of Adonis

The years glide by almost unnoticed, for nothing moves faster than the passage of time. Born of his own sister and grandfather and hidden in his mother's trunk, the baby is now a boy, now a full man, and more handsome than ever. He even arouses the passion of the goddess Venus herself. Venus falls in love with the beautiful young man and leaves her home and sanctuary to be with him. She even prefers his company to that of the gods of the heavens. She holds him close and makes love to him; he is her constant companion.

Venus warns her young lover. "Adonis, don't be foolish and go hunting with the other young men. Always fear the untamed beasts. Don't provoke those wild predators, for it is in their nature to attack and kill. Wild boars are especially fierce and dangerous with their lethal tusks. I myself fear and hate them all." And, with these words, the goddess left her young lover. She ascended into the air on the backs of her sacred swans.

Adonis ignored her warnings. As fate would have it, his faithful dogs caught the scent of a wild boar and gave chase, rousting it from its lair. Rushing from the woods and fleeing the boar, Adonis turned and struck the boar with his spear. Immediately, the wild beast dug the bloody spear out with its curved tusks. Now, provoked, the boar turned on the terrified Adonis, who ran for his life. The boar sank his deadly tusks deep into the young man's groin, hurling Adonis's body to the ground.

From a long way off, Venus heard the screams of the dying Adonis. When she saw her lover lying lifeless in a pool of his own red blood, she leaped down, tore at her clothes, and dug her nails into her breasts. Hurling threats at the death-bearing Fates, those awesome deities, she screamed, "You Fates will not get your way this time! Dear Adonis, you will have an eternal monument. Every year your loss will be recalled. All Nature will mourn. Your red life's blood will be changed into a flower. Just as you, O Persephone, are remembered each spring with the return of the sweet scented mint, I shall do the same for Adonis."

Saying this, Venus sprinkled the blood of Adonis with the sweet nectar of the gods. His blood immediately foamed with bubbles, just like burning lava. In less than an hour, a flower sprang up of a blood red color, the same shade as the rind of the pomegranate, which hides its regenerative seeds inside. But the life cycle of this flower is short. The winds blow the fragile petals that quickly fall to the earth. We call it the windflower, or red anemone.

At the peak of perfection in July, peaches are plucked from the trees and corn is harvested for consumption. So, too, Adonis was cut down in the fullness of life. July is bittersweet. It is the month to savor abundance and to anticipate death. In the myth, Adonis's death beckons us to recall the passing of our full powers, best work, and relationships at their greatest intensity. Likewise, the solar cycle echoes the death of Adonis by beginning a movement away from full light on a course toward darkness. July is a transitional month, as we enter the seasons of separation, decline, and ultimate death. This myth teaches that all fullness must pass and that death is painful, poignant, tragic, but also, like the red anemone, bears the promise of a new beginning in nature's cycle.

RITES AND RITUALS OF JULY

The Cycle of Life

In this month, we honor Adonis at the Adonia, a most poignant and powerful rite. For the women of antiquity, this rite brought the myth "to life" and allowed the participants (this rite was restricted to women) to experience symbolically the life/death cycle. The ritual of the Adonia provided a means for Greek and Roman women to express their deepest feelings, to plant a seed, to water and nurture, to grieve and mourn communally, and to sing the hymn for rebirth. This festival was held in July, in the hot summer months when plants wither and die.

ADONIS

ADONIA

Female members of the household climbed to their rooftops to enact the Adonia and to plant the "gardens of Adonis." They placed shallow layers of soil in potsherds or baskets and planted the seeds of such fast-growing crops as fennel, lettuce, wheat, or barley.

The women tended their "gardens of Adonis" for eight days. During this time, because the seedlings were exposed to the long sunny hours, they germinated well and grew quickly. After the eighth day the women left the gardens unattended, and the young plants soon withered and died under the sun's scorching rays. Women would come together, then mourn the shriveled seedlings, wailing and crying in unison.

Women in antiquity also made puppets or effigies of Adonis, the God of Living and Dying. They would make small replicas of coffins and place the effigies inside. An ancient Athenian remarked that the streets were lined with these small "coffins of Adonis" in midsummer.

Adonis was nurtured by the water nymphs, growing and thriving under their diligent maternal care to manhood, "more beautiful than ever." Adonis was truly in the fullness of life, a ripe fruit ready for plucking by Venus. As the embodiment of vegetation, he too came to fulfillment in July.

MODERN RITUAL FOR ABUNDANCE

Select fruit locally from your own fruit tree or a farmer's market. Chose the biggest plumpest peach, plum, or bunch of grapes, whatever is ripe in your locale in July. Figs are especially valued this month. Put out a glass bowl of fresh fruit as an offering. An appropriate libation would be the juice squeezed from any seasonal fruit. The juice of the earth's bounty was returned to the soil with prayers and thanksgiving.

Harvest began in July in ancient Rome when farmers were advised to bring in the barley, beans, fragrant fruits, and vegetables. There was great activity on the farm, family members working long hours in the orchards and fields gathering in the crops. This is a month to revel in the fullness of the crops, the animals that have grown strong, the children who flourish, the family that thrives.

We too must learn to relish the moment when things are going well and enjoy the beauty in life—a life in full bloom like midsummer flowers. Venus knew how to enjoy her moments with the beautiful Adonis. But more important, this goddess knew when she beheld beauty. And she was not distracted from lavishing attention upon Adonis. Knowing when we behold beauty is vital. Acknowledging and rejoicing in the moment is essential. We need to take a good look at ourselves and find our own beauty. It is there! Let us taste deeply of our own successes. We are to go over all the things, no matter how trivial, that we have done well, that we have nurtured to growth—our children, our job, our relationships. We must cherish the wonderful memories and moments when all seemed to go well. Like Venus, we must allow ourselves this luxury. Let us ever remain in awe of beauty.

Destruction and Endings

Things come to an end in July. July is a turning point marking the halfway point in the year. It has been six month since we began our journey together with the sun following its course till midsummer. We have reached the apex, the longest day, and now we change our course. Our path now leads in the other direction, to the decline of daylight, the death of vegetation, the hibernating period, and the onset of the dark cold months of winter. July teaches us about things coming to fruition and endings, some not so gentle.

HYMN TO ADONIS

Sung at the Adonia in Alexandria, Egypt

In this passage from a short play by Theocritus (third century B.C.E.), two women from Alexandria, Egypt, Praxinoe and Gorgo, were invited to attend the Adonia as celebrated in the hot summer at the house of the Pharaoh's wife. The events in the play describe the ritual fairly accurately. With bare bosoms and hair flowing down, the women would throw seedlings together with an effigy of the god Adonis into a river, spring, or ocean. Only after *The Hymn to Adonis* was sung could the women rejoice.

THE HYMN TO ADONIS, THE DYING GOD

Honor Adonis with all things beautiful. Beside him lie all ripe fruits that the tall trees bear, and delicate gardens, arrayed in baskets of silver, and the golden flasks are full of incense of Syria. And all the dainty cakes that women fashion in the kneading-tray, mingling colors manifold with the white wheat flour, and those they make of sweet honey and soft oil. . . .

In Adonis's rosy arms the Lady of Cypris lies, and he in hers. A bridegroom of eighteen or nineteen years is he, his kisses are not rough, the golden down being still upon his lips. And now good-night to Cypris, in the arms of her lover. But in the morning, we will all of us gather with the dew, and carry him forth among the waves that break upon the beach, and with hair loosed, bosoms bare, and robes falling to the ankles, will we begin our shrill sweet song.

Be gracious to us now, dear Adonis, and throughout the coming year. Dear to us has thine advent been, Adonis, and dear shall it be when thou comest again.

July 5, III Nones

POPLIFUGIA

Poplifugia literally means "Flight of the People" and is the only holiday of such importance in the entire year to be celebrated before the Nones. This most ancient ritual, was so old that it was not fully understood by the Romans of the historic period. Apparently the powers that were released this month were so fearful that the citizens had to flee. The ritual connected with the Poplifugia took place on the Field of Mars, traditionally associated with the military and aggressive action.

July 7, Nones

C O N S U S

On the Nones of July, July 7, an underground altar to Consus, the God of the Store Bin, was exposed and an offering made. The altar is said to lie under the southeastern turn in the Circus Maximus. (See August 21, December 15.)

It's July and the sun burns hot. Temperatures soar and the days are long. Lack of rain, too much sun, too late a harvest mean a destroyed crop. The past months of planting and nurturing the crops to fruition is coming to an abrupt end. They must be picked at the moment of ripeness, or the hot sun will burn the crops and destroy everything. Timing is essential! If the harvest is too late, the crops wither on the vine under the blazing heat. July demands aggressive action. July can also bring destruction.

We also have the power to destroy and we must face this. It was the women who, by not watering the plants at the Adonia, caused them to shrivel. It was a wild boar that castrated the beautiful Adonis. And wild animal power is often associated with aggressive female power—the power of Diana, not Venus, as told in this myth of the Calydonian Boar.

The king of Calydonia offered the firstfruits to all at harvesttime, to Ceres and Bacchus and Minerva and rural deities, but not to Diana, Goddess of the Wild and Untamed.

Anger can also move the Gods; and Diana was angered. "I will not endure this insult," she said. "Although I am not honored, it will not be said that I am unavenged."

In her anger, Diana sent rampaging across the fields of Greece a wild boar the size of a bull. His eyes burned with blood and fire, his neck stood stiff and rigid, and his stiff bristles stood out like spear shafts. Giving thunderous deep grunts, he spewed hot foam over his hide as he ran. His tusks were equal in size to an elephant's, and lightning bolts flamed out his mouth.

The grass was burned and shriveled beneath his fiery breath. He trampled the grain growing in the fields, he ravaged the fully ripe crops; he destroyed the vines hanging heavy with grapes, and the hardy olive trees that endure most anything. He vents his rage on the cattle too.

The people flee in all directions . . . (Ovid Metamorphoses 8.279)

White-hot rage and destruction is what July is also about. We acknowledge our destructive side. We have rage and we can destroy. We must be truthful—there are times when we wish to zap someone with forked tongues of lightning flashing from our mouth. Or shrivel an object with a look of burning hatred. Or just stomp on all those who have done us an injustice. And anger can also move us. "There are times when it becomes imperative to release a rage that shakes the skies. There is a time—even though these times are very rare, there is definitely a time—to let loose all the firepower one has," states Pinkola Estés. "It has to be in response to a serious offense; the offense has to be big and against the soul or spirit. . . . There is definitely a right time for full-bore rage. . . . And it is right. Right as rain" (Pinkola Estés, 361).

Full-bore rage may be what you need! Often anger is generalized and without focus, without a face. Through the rituals of July, women of antiquity could release the rage with control when they symbolically slapped a slave or beat men with branches from a fig tree. July was the right time to identify with that aspect of Diana or the searing, destructive, aggressive component of solar power. It is a month for ritualized rage.

JUNO CAPROTINAE

Juno Caprotinae was worshiped on this day, when women offered sacrifice to her beneath a wild fig tree. Both slave women and freeborn women attended this rite, and fig tree branches became part of the sacred objects. Also, "milky juice of the fig tree was offered"—the juice from figs was offered to the goddess in place of milk. The mothering aspect of tree is apparent (Varro *De Lingua Latina* 6.18).

July 7, NONES

FERIAE ANCILLARUM

The ancient and unusual ritual called Feriae Ancillarum, or Feast of the Serving Women, was so old that its origin was forgotten. At the festival, booths made of fig tree branches were set up on the outskirts of Rome. The *ancilliae*, or slave women, dressed in their best, attacked young men of free birth, beating them and engaging in ritualized battles with boughs from the fig tree.

MODERN RITUAL TO VENT RAGE

We too can vent anger and rage in ways acceptable by current standards. Fill a pinata or paper bag not with candy and sweets, but with messages on paper listing the things you hate or the names of people who make you mad. Seal the pinata with a prayer to Juno or Diana, any goddess who serves as protectress, suspend it where you have room, and whack away! This may seem silly, but it is very cathartic.

Madness and Prophecy

Apollo, the Sun God, can drive us all a little mad in July. It is hot and things fry. The power of the sun cannot be ignored. During July your skin turns red and blisters without proper protection, and your eyes ache from the intense sunlight. It is difficult to work outside and remain focused without water and shade. Apollo's searing heat can drive you mad in July. He also raged at the Cumaean Sibyl. As Sun God, Apollo was also the God of Wisdom and Prophecy.

July 6–13, I NONES–III IDES

GAMES OF APOLLO

Apollo was strictly a Greek god. The Romans adopted the cult, and the Games of Apollo were established for July during the late third century B.C.E. during the wars with Hannibal. Because of the popularity of the games, by 44 B.C.E. seven days had been set aside to honor Apollo. The games in the Circus, chiefly horse races, lasted two days, while plays and stage productions carried on for five days.

It was customary to put garlands all over the home, and for the woman of the house to lead all in prayers. A big feast was held during this time. Tables and couches were set up in the entranceways of the houses and the front doors were left open during the banquets.

The Cave of the Sibyl is located in the ancient town of Cumae, just north of Naples, where it can be found directly under the Cumaean acropolis and temple of Apollo. Her cave is an extraordinary place, a site full of ancient power and wisdom, for Sibyls of antiquity (and there were over ten) were prophetesses. For all the ages, Apollo literally presses down upon this prophetess. Deep in her cavern, her home, it is somehow easier to comprehend that enlightenment and inner knowledge often come from very dark places. One grows from the other, as these forces work in tandem. And it takes a wild, intuitive woman to voice them; being filled with the divine is often linked to madness.

SIBYL OF CUMAE

The rocky citadel had been colonized by [Greeks] and one side of it had been hollowed out to form a vast cavern into which led a hundred broad shafts, a hundred mouths, from which streamed as many voices giving the responses of the Sibyl. [The Trojans] had reached the threshold of the cavern when the virgin priestess [the Sibyl] cried. Now is the time to ask your destinies. It is the god. The god is here. At that moment as she spoke in front of the doors, her face was transfigured, her color changed, her hair fell in disorder about her head and she stood there with heaving breast and her wild heart bursting in ecstasy. She seemed to grow in stature and speak as no mortal had ever spoken when the god came to her in his power and breathed upon her.

But the priestess was still in wild frenzy in her cave and still resisting Apollo. The more she tried to shake her body free of the great god, the harder he strained upon her foaming mouth, taming the wild heart and molding her by his pressure. And now the hundred huge doors of her house opened of their own accord and gave her answer to the winds. . . . With these words from her shrine the Sibyl of Cumae sang her fearful riddling prophecies, her voice booming in the cave as she wrapped the thought in darkness, while Apollo shook the reins upon her in her frenzy and dug the spurs into her flanks. The madness passed. The wild words died upon her lips. (Virgil Aeneid 6.1–100)

MODERN RITUAL TO APPEASE THE SUN GOD, APOLLO

Cool off! Prepare a picnic with herbs, fruit, wine, and summer's bounty. Eat outdoors if you can. Leave your windows or door open to let the Sun God enter your home. Here is a recipe that is great for the hot summer months:

GRANITA DI LIMONE: LEMON ICE *(6 to 8 servings)*

$^2/_3$ cup sugar

2 cups and 2 tablespoons water

3 large lemons, juiced and strained to remove pulp and seeds

Bring the water to a boil, add the sugar and stir well until dissolved. Let the sugar mixture cool. Once cool, add lemon juice. Freeze in a metal ice cube tray. When the mixture begins to freeze and is mushy, stir it (about one and half to two hours). Stir again after one more hour. Freeze and serve.

As we enter the cave of the Cumaean Sibyl, the burning rays of the intense July sun give way to the somber cool shades of an underground chamber. This abrupt exchange between sunlight and darkness is a theme repeated throughout our journey into the cave. As pilgrims did several millennia ago, we find ourselves maneuvering down a passageway cut into living rock, cut by human hand thousands of years earlier. The sacred path moves through a corridor lit at intervals with natural sunlight streaming in from trapezoidal-shaped windows along the side. We walk from dark to light to dark again as we journey ahead, toward an unknown goal deep within the earth. The inner chamber we finally enter some four hundred yards from the entrance is not a tomb, but was the dwelling of a living person, the Cumaean Sibyl. This secret mysterious place resonates with Virgil's words.

> *You will see a virgin priestess foretelling the future in prophetic frenzy by writing signs and names on leaves. After she has written her prophecies on these leaves she seals them all up in her cave where they stay in their appointed order. But the leaves are so light that when the door turns in its sockets the slightest breath of wind dislodges them. The draft from the door throws them into confusion and the priestess never makes it her concern to catch them as they flutter round her rocky cave and put them back in order or join up the prophecies. So men depart without receiving advice and are disappointed in the house of the Sibyl. (Virgil Aeneid 3.441–54)*

Her prophecy, as with most oracles, was often ambiguous and interpretation left up to the individual seeking help. You asked your questions, sought your answers, and picked up your leaves. People often left disappointed.

Loss and Rebirth and Regeneration

July teaches us how to separate and let go of something that was dear to us, something that we nurtured to full growth. We have seen our crops to harvest, counted our losses, and must move on. The path of the sun is moving toward darkness, and we see the end of green leafy trees and warm days of sunlight, though still months off. We wail and grieve. Oh, how can this happen? Well it does. Nature gives us notice in July.

July 8, VIII IDES

V I T U L A

V I T U L A T I O

On July 8 the Vitulatio was celebrated, a festival in honor of the goddess Vitula. We are told by Macrobius (3.2.11) that after the Poplifugia, the Romans honored the goddess Vitula. She was the Goddess of Joy and Life—in fact her name comes from the word *vita,* or "life." On this day the goddess Vitula received the firstfruits of the earth which gave life (Virgil *Georgics* 3.77).

We mourn the loss of Adonis, the loss of fullness, and beauty, and on the level of family and relationships, changes that result in loss of intensity. Finally, we remember that communal grieving has great healing power, as seen in the women's lament for Adonis.

July 19, 21; XIV, XII KALENDS AUGUST

L A C U R I A

The Lacuria is a ritual that was held on two days, really dual rites. The rites took place in Rome at the Vial Salaria and the Tiber, where an ancient sacred grove of trees was located. The name Lacus means "grove of trees," and the ritual was to propitiate all those spirits that reside in trees. It was said that the money for this festival was derived from revenue made from public groves. This was especially relevant as this was the time in July to slash and burn, to clear land and fields. Trees were destroyed, then honored, and then land was cleared for new cultivation. There was a special prayer to be said by farmers before they cleared a grove of trees on their property.

PRAYER TO THE SPIRIT OF THE GROVE

Be thou god or goddess to whom this grove is dedicated, as it is thy right to receive a sacrifice of a pig for the thinning of this sacred grove, and to this intent, I or one at my bidding do it, may it be rightly done. To this end, in offering this pig to thee I humbly beg that thou will be gracious and merciful to me, my house and household, and to my children. Will you deign to receive this pig which I offer thee for this purpose? (Cato *De Agricultura* 139 LCL).

We can sing the hymn to the dying god Adonis, "Dear will it be when he comes again," and look ahead for next spring. From destruction comes new growth. But this may not be right away and months may go by, but all will be well. Patience and an inner sense that all will be well stem from belief in nature's regenerative cycle. This sacred knowledge is healing. Women in antiquity performed water rituals to heal, complete the cycle, and to confirm the Coming Again.

July 23, X KALENDS AUGUST

NEPTUNUS

NEPTUNALIA

Neptunus was the ancient Italic God of Water—most likely in the oldest times of freshwater or springwater. Neptunus protected all waterways and human activities linked to water. His festival was held in the hottest month, July. His counterpart was Salacia, Goddess of Leaping Water or Spring Water. Neptunus was also connected with Venilia, the Roman Goddess of Coastal Water, although neither Salacia nor Venilia had rituals of their own. On July 23, shady arbors were made of leaves for the worshipers, which undoubtedly helped protect them from the sun. An altar to Neptunus in the Circus Flamininus was dedicated on this day in the third century B.C.E. The offering and prayers to Neptunus were for a continued supply of water during the hottest days of the year.

July 25, VIII KALENDS AUGUST

FURRINA

FURRINALIA

Furrina, the Goddess of Springs and Wells, was also worshiped at this time. Her rite was most ancient and she had her own special priest. Furrina was worshiped in a grove on the Janiculum Hill (one of the seven hills of Rome) across the Tiber River near the Sublician Bridge. In fact, the cleft with a spring of water that was her sanctuary can still be visited today. She was such an ancient goddess, later Roman authors did not quite understand her. Varro says: "Honor was paid to her among the ancients, who established an annual sacrifice and assigned her a special priest. But her name is barely known, and even that to only a few" (Varro *De Lingua Latina* 6.19 LCL). She had been forgotten even in antiquity, overshadowed by the male counterpart Neptune.

July is the month to have faith and work to set things right for rebirth. Water is not only restorative, but essential in the heat of July. Since the oldest times, water has symbolized birth, healing, and renewal. The July rituals to Neptunus and Furrina, the Goddess of Springs, balance the scorching heat sent by Apollo.

MODERN RITUAL OF RESTORATION

Leave out bowls of water in the hot sun to evaporate; the transformation of water to air to rain replicates the natural life-giving cycle. An interesting ritual was performed at the end of the Eleusinian rite in September, yet it can be appropriate here:

- Take two earthen vessels, shallow bowls, or cups holding cool water.
- Set one to face the west and one to the east.
- Tip them over in turn, giving the earth a good drink.
- Face the sky and cry, "Rain!" Then, turn your face to the earth and cry, "Conceive!" (In Greek, these words rhyme, "Hye! Kye!")

The month ends with a celebration to *fortunae huiusque diei*, or the "Fortunes of This Day." *Fortuna huiusque diei* reminds us to be grateful and live in the day, the moment. We have truly realigned ourselves with the trees, the water, the earth. We prepare for the fall.

MODERN RITUAL OF THE ADONIA

The Adonia is a ritual that embodies the cycle of nature, which changes with the phases of growth, death, and expectation of rebirth. As you read the myth of Adonis, think of possible ways to adapt the ritual in a group that would provide meaning to you. Plant some seeds in pots with a scant amount of soil, water them until they begin to grown, then allow the young seedlings to wither and die in the direct rays of the hot July sun. Impart into the seedlings those beautiful and positive ideas, thoughts, or tokens of self-expression that have withered and died inside of you for lack of nurturing. Mourn them, each and every one. Then consider just how they can be reborn or reshaped to bring fulfillment to your life. End with only hopeful thoughts and sweet words. Celebrate renewal with an adaptation of an ancient recipe for the "Cakes of Adonis" (Dalby):

ITRIA: CAKES OF HONEY FROM ALEXANDRIA *(makes about 20 pieces)*

Itria were thin, sweet cakes made of sesame and honey, possibly served at the Adonia. (Athenaeus 646d)

$1/2$ cup sesame seeds $1/2$ cup sugar
$1/2$ cup chopped walnuts $1/2$ cup water
$1/2$ cup clear honey

Roast the sesame seeds and nuts in the oven at 350 degrees until they turn slightly brown. Put the honey in a saucepan and bring to a boil. Let boil until very firm stage (about 250 degrees). Add nuts and seeds. Butter a shallow baking tray and spread the mixture on it. Allow to cool and serve.

July ends. "Now the air burns white with flaming heat." (Ovid Metamorphosis *I.119)*

AUGUST
THE MONTH TO REAP

Prayer to Diana

Let us sing to Diana
Lady of the mountains and green forests,
Hidden glens, and rushing rivers.
Mothers in the pains of childbirth call you Lucina;
You are called mighty Trivia,
And Moon with your glowing light.
You, Goddess, by your monthly menstrual cycle
measure out a year's journey.
You fill full the rustic home of the farmer with good fruits.
By whatever name you chose, Be You Holy!
With kind help, keep us safe. (Catullus Poem 34)

Rural Menologia
Sun in Leo
31 days
Nones: August 5
Daylight: 13 hours
Darkness: 11 hours

→>•<←

This busy month ancient Roman farmers were to cut straw, build hay stacks, harrow and plough the land, collect leaf fodder, mow irrigated fields, prepare stakes, harvest the wheat and other produce, store the crops, and burn the coarse part of the flax. (Menologia)

August is the hottest of months; the sun's rays scorch the earth. The ground bakes beneath our feet; the heat broils our senses. It is definitely the time to retreat to the sea or the mountains in search of cool breezes and pleasant nights. Imagine hiking over mountainous terrain and coming upon a lush green valley, watered by a natural spring and shaded with tall leafy trees dipping their branches to the stream's edge. Who wouldn't race down the grassy slopes and plunge headlong into the cool water? Who could pass by the gurgling spring without taking a deeply satisfying drink on a blistering hot August day?

Our focus shifts this month from Adonis, July's dying and reborn God of Vegetation, to the absolute power, the truly creative power of the Divine Feminine. The month of August is ruled by female deities, goddesses who demand our devotion. Diana, manifest as the Great Mother and Creatrix, embodies the mystery and ultimate power inherent in nature. Mother Earth's gifts, the fauna and flora she has created and has given to us for sustenance, are being hunted and harvested in August. While we mortals take from the earth, we need to be ever vigilant and mindful of the natural process. We must respect Mother Earth, hold her in awe, and not defile her. Actaeon defiled Diana—he saw the goddess exposed. He had to die.

Diana and Actaeon

Do you question the cause of Actaeon's death? Is it a crime to stray from the path? It was not his fault, but it was his fate.

It happened on a mountain, the home to many wild animals—a popular place to hunt. The noonday sun directly overhead made the heat unbearable, and it was difficult to find shade. Young Prince Actaeon called out to his friends in the hunting party, "Our nets and spears are dripping with the blood of our prey. We have been fortunate already today in the hunt. Let's return home, and start out fresh again tomorrow. The Sun God, Apollo, is now highest in the sky, the ground bakes in the intense heat. Stop tracking your prey and bring back home those hunting nets."

The men did as he said.

There was a valley nearby, densely overgrown with pine trees and prickly cypress trees. It was called Gargaphie, sacred sanctuary to Diana, Goddess of the Hunt. Here in this hidden valley was a shady grotto never before seen by human eyes. Nature had carved out from living rock a natural arch that looked just like a bridge. A small stream gurgled loudly, rushing downward over the rocks, and spilling into a pool that was lined with green grassy banks.

The goddess Diana, when tired of the hunt, often came here to bathe naked in the clear cool water. On this particular day, she came to her sacred grotto accompanied by her band of faithful nymphs. She handed over her hunting spear, quiver, and unstrung bow to a nymph for safe-keeping. Another nymph picked up the clothes she threw down. Two more nymphs untied the sandals from her divine feet. The nymph Crocale, known to be an expert hairdresser, tied up the goddess's long hair, which fell below her divine neck. Others brought large urns and filled them with cool water to pour over the goddess.

So while Diana bathed in her private pool, the hunter Actaeon was heading for home. Yet he lost his way and became disoriented, wandering unknowingly into Diana's grove. His fate led him there! As soon as he entered the sacred spot with the bubbling spring water, the nymphs caught site of him. They tried to cover their naked breasts. Their shrill cries resonated throughout the grove. Gathering around Diana, they tried in vain to hide her with their own bodies. But the goddess was far taller—their heads barely reached her neck. Diana blushed the color of rosy red clouds at dawn, as she stood completely naked and in full view. She turned her back on Actaeon, glaring at him over her shoulder.

She wished for her bow and arrows, but all that she had for defense was the water. She quickly scooped up a handful of water and splashed it in the young hunter's face. As she sprayed him, she shouted a curse that sealed his doom. "Now you can brag to everyone that you have seen me naked—if you are able to speak."

On his head where the water drops fell long antlers of a stag suddenly began to grow. His neck extended, his ears became pointed, his hands turned into hooves, his arms changed into long legs, and his skin became a soft brown spotted hide. Actaeon fled, wondering why he now could run so nimbly, until he glanced at his reflection in the crystal clear pool of water. "What is happening to me?" he tried to scream, but no words come out. The only noise he could make was a groan, yet tears ran down his deerlike cheeks, for his mind was the only thing that Diana did not change.

As he was deciding what next to do, he saw his own dogs, keen-scented hounds trained by him to hunt and kill the prey. Hot on the trail, the dog pack went wild with the scent of prey. They give chase, pursuing their quarry over steep cliffs and rocks where there was no path. Actaeon fled across the land that he had once hunted. He ran from his own dogs. He tried to call to them, "I am your master Actaeon, obey me." But he had no voice. The air was filled with their loud barks. One sank his fangs in the stag's back, another hung into the shoulder. The whole pack attacked the prey, digging their teeth into his body, ripping his flesh. Actaeon groaned and uttered a last sound—neither human nor animal—that echoed off the mountain peaks.

He fell to his knees as if he were praying, facing his comrades in silence, beseeching them with his eyes. But his friends and fellow hunters didn't recognize Actaeon. They sicced the dog pack on the helpless stag. Deceived by the deer's form, the dogs attacked from all sides. Plunging their teeth into his flesh, they ripped apart their master. Not until Actaeon lay dead from this savage attack by his own hunting dogs was the rage of the quiver-bearing goddess Diana appeased.

Actaeon was a strong, willful young man in the prime of his life doing manly things with his comrades, raiding the mountain forests for prey. Only the midday heat of the summer month slowed him down, at a time of day when the sun burned hottest and no shade could be found. The ploughed fields no longer held crops, for they had already been harvested. The soil underfoot was baked hard and dry from the August sun. Returning home, Actaeon wandered off from his comrades and dog pack.

He stumbled upon a lush green valley and did not hesitate to climb down. As Fate would have it, Actaeon came upon the remote sanctuary of the goddess Diana, a holiest of holy spots unseen by mortal eyes. He certainly saw the nymphs and heard their screams first, yet he was young. He did not have the wisdom or knowledge to look away and flee. Instead, he peered over the nymphs and saw the great goddess Diana naked; he beheld her divinity.

Actaeon was killed, sacrificed to his own hounds. This mortal youth had trespassed onto the sacred sanctuary and beheld the divine and naked majesty of the goddess Diana. But, who is this goddess? According to Joseph Campbell, "Diana was a manifestation of that goddess-mother of the world" (Campbell, 62). Young Actaeon was not prepared for the sight of the divine in the raw; he saw things he should never have seen. And no one lives to see and reveal the secret of the Divine Feminine, Mother of the World.

It is not difficult to see what enticed Actaeon to enter that cool valley. That is what August does to you. Out in the sun all day, your skin turns red and blisters, your eyes water, you think you are going to die—and you seek relief. Not much lives in this intense heat, crops wither and die, animals seek shade. The Sun God, Apollo, rules. Ah, for a drink of cool spring water, to lie down at the edge of a mountain stream in the moist green grasses, to gaze up through the leafy shady trees—you feel as though you are born again.

Cool water, naked female bodies, a moist valley restricted to women, water gushing from a mysterious underground source—this is the sacred sanctuary of the great goddess Diana. This is a life-giving place of Birth, and a place known only to women. Actaeon had no right to be here, no right to see the Divine Mother in her divine sanctuary—he beheld the secret. He had to die to ensure the secret, and Diana did not hesitate. The power and the mystery of the Divine Feminine, the Mother of the World, was honored and held in awe.

The mid-month rites to Diana performed chiefly by women brought the worshipers in touch with the mysterious and awesome power of the earth—the power of the Creatrix. Diana is the ultimate protectress of the Divine Feminine. In the myth, we see Diana as Mother of Earth, her bounty and gift in the form of the animals hunted, and the death of Actaeon as one of the animals. He returns to the earth. August also marks the end of the growing period. It is now time for the harvest and the hunt in order to store sufficient food for the coming winter. Female deities take prominence this month, drawing our attention to the fact that female power has long been associated to the soil. The goddesses worshiped this month and the themes in the myth are interwoven with nature's cycle and the harvest month of August.

RITES AND RITUALS OF AUGUST

Protecting the Feminine

The goddess Diana teaches us the sanctity of the Divine Feminine, for which she is an assertive advocate and protectress. This is a lesson we should all take to heart.

August 1, KALENDS

S P E S

On the Kalends in August, a temple to Spes, or "Hope" (which now lies under the church of S. Nicola in Carcere), was dedicated in Rome during the Punic Wars of the fourth century B.C.E, although the cult was older. A public rite to the deity Spes was carried out at the temple every year on this day. She is often referred to as Bona Spes, or Good Hope. "If things are bad now, pray to the goddess Spes, so that in the future they will not be bad" (Latin proverb).

In art, the goddess Spes is shown holding an opening flower while she lifts up the hem of her skirt as if in haste to flee. These images seem appropriate, since hope can also be fleeting.

We should remember her as Diana Luna or Diana Lucifera, the Moon Goddess. We should remember her as Diana Opifera, Diana the Aid Bringer. We should remember her as Diana Venatrix, Diana the Huntress and Mistress of the Wild Animals. We should remember her as Diana/Hecate in the cypress grove. We should remember her as Virgin Goddess who needs no man.

151

Diana was in her most ancient guise, Italic Goddess of the Earth, Woods, and Groves. She was also honored as Moon Goddess, Virgin Goddess, Protectress of Childbirth, and Death Goddess. No wonder she was especially revered by women and associated with female powers. Her most famous cult site was in Nemi, some fifteen miles south of Rome, and her special day was August 13, or the Ides of August at full moon.

MODERN RITUAL TO HONOR THE FEMININE

Diana was the goddess to share your secrets with, the wildest fantasies, the prayer for a healthy happy family or success in a male world. She knows something of this! Women left small messages to Diana written on ribbons and tied to a fence at the sanctuary of Nemi. Diana also cured your ills, and numerous small statuettes of body parts have been found in many of her shrines. In Sicily, today, breads are baked in the shape of arms, feet, legs, hands, and other body parts, a custom from antiquity. Instead of bread dough, I prefer store-bought cookie dough, which works quite well. If you feel pain or aches somewhere in your body, bake up an appendage and offer it to Diana as a votive. And, for Diana's sake, at the full moon, wash your hair and tuck some flowers behind your ears— a wild touch for a wild woman and goddess!

Nemi is unique and sacred. The Latin word *nemus* means "a sacred wood or grove." The round shape of the lake (it is actually in a volcanic crater) and the moon's reflection on dark nights caused the ancients to refer to it as Diana's mirror.

In the Arrician valley, there is a lake surrounded by shady forests,
Held sacred by a religion from the olden times . . .
On a long fence hang many pieces of woven thread,
and many tablets are placed there as grateful gifts to the goddess.

Often does a woman whose prayers Diana answered
With a wreath of flowers crowning her head,
Walk from Rome carrying a burning torch. . . .
There a stream flows down gurgling over its rocky bed,
I have often drunk it in; but only in small sips.

(Ovid Fasti 3.265–75)

August 5, NONES

SALUS

At Rome, a public sacrifice was made to goddess Salus. Salus is the goddess associated with safety, health, and welfare. An offering on the hilltop shrine to Salus ensured health and safety to the devout. This goddess was in earliest times an agricultural deity, as the health and success of the harvest was crucial to survival.

Salus was shown on coins feeding a sacred snake from a *patera*, or ritual plate; she held a scepter in her other hand. In some depictions, she is shown holding sheaves of wheat, most likely the more ancient image.

August 12, II IDES

LYCHNAPSIA

The Lychnapsia is the celebration of the birthday of the goddess Isis. This rite, added later to the Roman calendar, came from Egypt and involved the use of lamps.

Diana served as a protectress of women. She helped in childbirth and brought aid to those in need. She was known as Diana Opifera, or Diana Bringer of Aid. Women wrote down on tablets special messages and prayers when seeking help from Diana Opifera. In seeking Diana's aid in healing and fertility, they also left terra-cotta images of themselves, their loved ones, and body parts such as eyes, faces, and uteri.

DIANA

On these blistering hot summer days in mid-August, Roman women performed the rituals of Diana. "'Twas the season when the vault of heaven bends its most scorching heat upon the earth . . . and now the day had come when the torch smoke rises from Trivia's [Diana's] grove . . . and the [torch] lights twinkle on her lake" (Statius *Silvae* 3.1.55–57 LCL). On this day, we know that all women made a special practice of washing their hair (Plutarch *Roman Quaestiones* 100, LCL). Then in gratitude, women wearing wreaths of flowers in their hair and carrying torches made a procession to the sacred grove and sanctuary at Nemi. We know that they sought help from Diana and wrote their messages on tablets left at the site. Women grateful to Diana's guidance and protection throughout the year honored this goddess. There they conducted nocturnal rituals to the goddess, lining the lake with a ring of burning torches. They left votive offerings, clay stags in memory of Actaeon, hand-sculpted models of uteri, or statuettes of mother and child. Diana was a woman's goddess.

On this day, "Diana herself sets garlands on her faithful dogs and polishes her darts and lets the wild beasts go free . . ." (Statius *Silvae* 3.1.59). All slaves were freed from their regular work. In fact Diana's rite was one of the few that slaves could attend. Women of all classes were free that day to attend the rites of Diana at Nemi. Propertius, a Roman poet of the first century C.E., bemoans his lover's attending the rites:

Ah, if you would only walk here in your leisure hours.
But we cannot meet today,
When I see you hurrying in excitement with a burning torch
To the grove of Nemi where you
Bear light in honor of the goddess Diana. (2.32.7–16)

A woman's privacy should be held sacred. Those things that we own ourselves, our bodies, our feelings, and soulful musings, can be very fragile and vulnerable. When we need to retreat to a sacred place, whether it is "a room of our own," a quiet introspective moment at work, or a warm bath, our privacy must be respected. This is sacred time and restorative time when we can get back in touch with our feminine selves, be honest, and expose our true feelings and thoughts. We need these moments to glory in our wondrous female bodies and tap into our wild feminine intuitive nature—just as Diana did in her grotto. These small "retreats to the sacred grotto" are essential for well-being. Yet how often we neglect them!

Actaeon's intrusion was equivalent to a rape. The goddess was abused and violated. And her first response of shame quickly changed to rage and revenge—she looked for her bow and quiver of arrows. This goddess did not blame herself or allow the outrage to go unavenged. Again, we have much to learn from Diana. Women often feel guilty and passive when abused; we think, perhaps we did something to bring on the violation. We too often fear seeking vengeance and taking assertive action. We must learn to actively defend our wild female side and not allow intrusion or abuse. For one day each summer, the women of Rome retreated to the sacred grove, joined with the goddess Diana, and honored their wild, sacred female nature.

CREATING A SACRED AND PRIVATE SANCTUARY

A very private and soulful sanctuary in a hidden grotto with a small stream bubbling over the rocks and green lush banks is alluring to the senses and the soul. Diana had Gargaphie, her sacred sanctuary, and we also can create a most private retreat in nature. If we are lucky to have a garden, then we can truly create a cool and shaded retreat from all the daily cares and concerns. We can make a place of comfort and nourishment, a private and safe site for body and soul.

In lieu of our own physical retreat, we can create a private sanctuary by visualizing a magical garden. Then, by springing from our imagination, desire, and personal experience, our private place will truly be able to bring solace and replenish our spirits.

- First, think deeply about places in nature where you have been. Which of these inspired or moved you? Do you know why? What feelings do you wish to evoke in your sanctuary?
- Imagine standing at the entrance to your private space. What attracts you to it, beckoning you to enter? Is it quite shady or are there patches of filtered sunlight?

- Is there an enticing spot to sit or lie down? Where are these and what do they look like?
- Imagine the sound of water playing over the rocks. What water features would be there?
- What plants envelope this space? Describe the colors of the flowers and blossoms. Which are favorites and what are the planting patterns?
- Imagine the variety of wildlife attracted to this natural place. Think of the songbirds, the vibrant colored butterflies, the small lizards, rabbits, or deer—Diana's special animal.
- Soak in the sounds, smells, and sensations of this natural retreat that is yours and yours alone. Perhaps you could approximate such a natural retreat in your own backyard, or a much modified mini-sanctuary in a planter on your balcony. A painting can also capture the essence of this magical place, elevating your spirits with the mere suggestion of a wild natural shelter, a private place. (McDowell, 30)

The Gifts of the Earth

Thanks was given for an abundant harvest in August, with many rites honoring various aspects of the harvest—the vintage, the storing of the grain and crops, the picking the fruit from the trees. The god Vertumnus, or Season Changer, was the God of Autumn; his marriage to Pomona, the Goddess of Fruit, was indeed a marriage made in the heavens.

August 13, IDES

VERTUMNUS AND POMONA

Vertumnus was an ancient Etruscan deity whose cult was brought to Rome, where he had a temple on the northwest part of the Aventine in an ancient laurel grove. His name may originate in the Latin word "to change," *vertere*. Hence he may have been a shape changer. He was a harvest deity at an early time and is usually shown surrounded by the bountiful harvest. He always got the firstfruits, the first purple grapes, the first yellow corn, the first red cherries, green cucumbers, orange gourds, and all that bloomed in the meadow.

Vertumnus as Autumn is shown in a Pompeian wall painting as a young male crowned with vine leaves and bunches of grapes, holding a basket of fruit and vegetables. His wife Pomona, the Goddess of Fruit, was shown with a basket of luscious harvest crops.

Diana was the Mother Goddess of the wild animals and the hunt. It was she who gave the deer and wild animals as life-giving gifts to mortals, gifts necessary for survival in the oldest times of hunting and gathering. She was the Creatrix, and from her gifts of the hunt, mortals could feed. In an agrarian society, her life-giving gifts were the grains, fruits, and vegetables, the cultivated crops. Ploughing and sowing were equivalent to begetting, as we saw in March and May; then came the nurturing and growing months of June and July, when earth's bounty ripened to fruition. The hot summer month of August was harvest time and a time of endings.

Mother Earth sacrifices her crops so that mortals can eat; she sacrifices her animals to feed humankind. This is the ultimate gift of the Divine Feminine, the Creatrix. We mortals have taken the best from earth; we have hunted and harvested. Praise be to the earth.

In the myth, Actaeon was young and hot-blooded; he did not know to set limitations and he certainly overstepped the boundaries. He paid the ultimate price for not realizing this and obeying earth's dictates. These limits and boundaries were in fact set and determined by Diana, Mother of All, the Earth Goddess. You take in the hunt only what you need to feed yourself and never glory in the bloody slaughter of animals. Excess in the form of the slaughter of animals for sheer pleasure and bravado is stepping over the limit, presumptuous of Mother Earth's gifts. Ironically, Actaeon came to understand the great gift the deer gave to mortals in sacrificing his life. Yet the killing of this particular stag was not necessary, for the hunters had taken their full share already.

JUPITER AND VENUS
VINALIA RUSTICA

At this second festival to wine in the year (the first was held in April) both Jupiter and Venus were honored. The first wine festival celebrated the opening of the fall vintage and tasting. This festival in August, the Vinalia Rustica, held in the countryside, was to protect the growing grapes and announce the upcoming vintage, when it was auspicious to harvest the grapes.

Offerings to Venus included incense, myrtle, mint, and bands of rushes hidden in a cluster of roses. She was worshiped in temples and also in sacred gardens. The rustic Vinalia was held in August and is in honor of Venus, because on this day the goddess is venerated and those who tend kitchen gardens and farm gardens rest from their work, for it is thought that all gardens are under the tutelage of Venus.

We also must respect the earth and all living creatures. It was only a twist of fate, an instant, that altered Actaeon's perception. Abusing the earth and the environment is not just wrong, it is a sacrilege and defamation of the divine. We mortals are an integral part of the natural cycle; by polluting, hunting, destroying nature and her gifts we destroy ourselves. Actaeon came to understand this too late for his survival; we must come to understand this before it is too late for our own.

August 21, X Kalends September

C O N S U S

C O N S U A L I A

The Consualia was held on this day in ancient Rome. Consus, a god of the storage bin of harvested grain, was honored on this day. Consus had an underground altar in the Circus Maximus where the chief priest and the Vestal Virgins officiated at his rite. Once the dirt had been removed from the underground altar, Consus was honored with sacrifice and the burnt offerings for the firstfruits. Horses and other animals were allowed to rest on this day, and garlands were hung around their necks. Consus had two other festivals, one in July and one in December, for the winter sowing of grain.

August 23, VIII Kalends September

O P S

Ops was honored on this day. She was a goddess with two festivals, the Opiconsivia, in two days on August 25, and the Opalia, in December. She was linked with Consus and is also called either Consiva or Opifera. Hers was a grain and harvest festival. Her oldest place of worship was in the ancient Forum at Rome.

MODERN RITUAL OF THANKSGIVING FOR THE EARTH'S BOUNTY

Harvest rituals and rites of thanksgiving are time-honored events held over the centuries by many peoples. Our own Thanksgiving comes later in November, but the harvest itself comes during these late summer and early fall months. The firstfruits, which can be gained from either hunting, fishing, gathering, or agriculture, are traditional offerings. In antiquity, "firstfruits" were either burned, submerged, or just left out in the open.

- Celebrate a thanksgiving by offering the "firstfruits." Set out a portion of the "firstfruits" that you either grow or seasonally purchase in a sacred spot, a household shrine, a natural spring, or a special place in your environment.
- Hold a feast and party, for this was of foremost importance to the rite.
- Always offer prayer first. This bountiful rite simply gives thanks for the growing season.

Harvest and Death

Mother Earth giving of herself at harvest is equivalent to death—the growing period has ended as the crops are ripped from her womb. The hunt and slaughter of her animals also ends the period of growth. This is all part of nature and essential to human survival. We need to eat! But, as everything dies, it returns to the earth and back to the womb. Upon his death, the young hunter Actaeon returned to the earth, back to the womb of the Mother. This is also part of the natural process, for eventually new growth and sustenance comes out of death. It is difficult to understand the death of a loved one, a family member, a friend, or even a dear pet. Yet death must occur and will never be hindered. It is comforting to equate the grave or tomb of the dead with the sacred womb of Mother Earth. The tomb as a womb is an ancient concept.

August 24, VII KALENDS SEPTEMBER

MUNDUS OPENED

A strange rite occurred three times a year, today, in October, and in November. It appears to have involved the dead and centered around the *mundus*, "pit." In fact there were two ritual pits, one that Romulus dug when he founded Rome and the other the *mundus Cereris*, or Pit of Ceres. The latter mundus, a vaulted ritual pit divided into two parts with a cover, was exposed on these three days. The lifting of the lid was equal to opening the Gates of the Underworld. The spirits of the dead, the *manes*, could emerge and roam the streets on these days. This was a very holy day and no business could be transacted, no battles fought, no taxes levied, no marriages take place. In most early times the pit may have been associated with harvest, as one author says that the *mundus* belongs to Ceres. In 1914, a vaulted pit was discovered on the Palatine Hill and may be this ancient and mysterious *mundus Cereris*.

The ancient Romans, at the height of harvest between all the thanksgiving rituals, also honored the Di Manes, or spirits of the underworld. It was in mid-August that the dead shades walked the earth. Lifting the lid of the mundus ("Pit") was equal to opening the Gates of the Underworld. The mundus was ritually opened during the harvest season, when crops were stored underground for the winter and the seed was preserved in bins beneath the earth for next spring's planting.

August 25, VI KALENDS SEPTEMBER

OPS

OPICONSIVIA

Ops, the Goddess of Plenty, had her own festival, the Opiconsivia, without Consus on this day. Her shrine could be entered only by the Vestal Virgins and the chief state priest, who wore a white veil. A special broad bronze vessel called a *praefericulum* was used. Some regard Ops as Terra, or Earth, an interesting association of "Plenty" and "Earth," and call her the mother of Juno, Ceres, and Vesta. She was worshiped at her shrine in the Regia, home of the king, because she gave humans all the resources needed for survival, *omnes ops*. Her shrine at an early time may have been a communal storage area or larder of the king. It housed the fruits of the earth and was attended by the Vestals.

The correct and proper way to invoke her is to touch the earth with your hand and pray. In art she is seen sitting on a throne with a scepter, globe, and sheaves of wheat.

August 27, IV KALENDS SEPTEMBER

VOLTURNUS

VOLTURNALIA

The Volturnalia was celebrated on this day and the cult was very ancient, so ancient the Roman authors of the first century C.E. knew little about Volturnus. He was considered the father of the Fountain Goddess, Juturna, whose waters today feed into the fountain of Trevi. His name may be from the Latin *volvere*, "to roll," which would suggest a river or wind god. Perhaps he was a wind god who might damage the growing grape vines and needed to be propitiated.

So August comes to a close. "This is the month when the sun bends its scorching heat upon the earth. This is the season to honor Diana." (Statius Silvae 3.1.55–57)

SEPTEMBER

THE MONTH TO HARVEST LIFE

*One buries children, one gains new children, one dies oneself; and this people
take heavily, carrying earth to earth. But it is necessary to harvest life like
a fruit-bearing ear of grain.* (Euripides Hypsipyle *fragment 757*)

Rural Menologia
SUN IN VIRGO
30 DAYS
NONES: SEPTEMBER 5
DAYLIGHT: 12 HOURS
DARKNESS: 12 HOURS
EQUINOX

Ancient farmers were advised to paint the wine jars with pitch, pick apples, and loosen the soil around the roots of the trees. At the equinox, the farmers were to cut straw, harrow the ploughed land, and gather in fodder. (Menologia)

September, when the summer growing season is over and the harvest nears completion, is a month of endings. Although many days remain sunny and warm, the intense heat of summer is past and the first cooler days appear, as the sun continues its six-month journey toward the winter solstice and the hours of light are noticeably shorter approaching the equinox. A few leaves turn brown and fall from the trees, harbingers of the glorious, but so brief, display of nature's magnificent color before the dull tones of late fall and winter set in. In the Roman rustic calendar, September represented a quiet time for the busy farmer with the winding down of the harvest, for the summer fruits and vegetables had been picked and the sheaves of grain had been cut down. In the countryside, September was a time for thanksgiving. Wine or honey mixed with milk was poured directly into the ground as libation, and spontaneous dances and songs were offered to Ceres for a bounteous harvest by oak-leaf-crowned young men and women. September was also the month of grief and the time to mourn the loss.

In the agrarian calendar, the jubilation brought on by a bounteous harvest of summer crops now gave way to a sadness and preparation for the end. September is a month to acknowledge the end, and it is a time for closure. Yet this too is only part of the natural cycle. As in August, powerful goddesses prevail this month, but with a difference. The goddesses of September do not strike out, but instead serve as reminders of the eternal life cycle. These goddesses offer hope and restore faith.

The story I am about to tell has been retold and reenacted for thousands of years at countless secret rituals to the Greek goddess Demeter or Ceres, her Roman counterpart. There was a time long ago when men and women attended the rites to Demeter in September, marching from Athens to the small town called Eleusis, some fourteen miles northwest of Athens. What was it that drew them for the weeklong ceremony? What compelled them to take part in this ritual, the most famous mystery of the classical world, a rite no initiate could ever discuss openly for fear of death? We cannot answer that question with any certainty; we can only infer. Because this was a very solemn rite and the initiates took their oath seriously, no reliable source exists to describe the events in any detail. Thus, the rites of the Eleusinian Demeter have remained enigmatic—a mystery—for nearly three thousand years.

Let this sacred tale of mother and daughter, possibly the most powerful of all the classical myths, serve as an introduction to the Greater Eleusinian Mysteries, held in the last half of September, and to the Thesmophoria, which occurred shortly thereafter. This sacred and truly feminine myth delves deep into the earth, into nature, and into our psyches, drawing strength from ageless archetypes. This is a story of loss, grief, and suffering, and it is appropriate for September.

Originally an oral poem, the myth of Ceres and Persephone was written down sometime between 650 and 550 B.C.E. by an anonymous Greek bard. The version you will find here is Roman; it begins in Sicily near the modern town of Enna and was composed by Ovid in the first few years of the common era.

Ceres and Persephone

I must now tell you the story of the abduction of the Virgin. You will recognize it, but you will learn a few new things as well.

The land of Sicily lies to the south, an island surrounded by water. This is the cherished land of Ceres. She calls many cities her home in Sicily, but especially the lush town of Enna with its fertile soil. One day, Arethusa, the Nymph of Cool Waters, had invited all the Divine Mothers to her sacred spring. The golden-haired goddess Ceres came to the sacred rites, but her daughter Persephone wished instead to wander barefoot through the meadows of Enna that day. She planned to pick wildflowers with her girlfriends.

Now there is a special place in a valley near Enna, a place that is shady and wet, as it is sprayed by the mists of a tall waterfall. This magic place is dappled with all the colors and hues found in nature. The ground is covered with an array of beautiful wildflowers. As soon as she saw this magic place, Persephone called out to her girlfriends, "Come here quick and we can gather all the wildflowers we want to take home."

The young girls eagerly began to pick the flowers. One filled her basket with green herbs, another loaded her skirt with the flowers, arranging them in the bodice of her gown. One girl picked marigolds, another violets. One pinched off poppy flowers with her fingernails. Some girls liked the hyacinths, some amaranths, others fragrant thyme blossoms, or clover. Many young girls picked roses along with flowers that had no particular name. Persephone herself chose delicate golden crocuses and white lilies. She became so absorbed in gathering wildflowers that little by little she wandered off from her companions. As chance would have it, no one followed her. It was then that he spied her.

Uncle Dis, Lord Hades of the Underworld, came and swiftly abducted her, carrying her off to his dark realm on the backs of his blue-black horses. Of course, she cried out, "Io, dearest Mother, I am being carried away!" She had even ripped the bodice of her gown. At once, a road to the Dark Realm opened up for Dis, because his horses could no longer bear the bright light. When her friends had filled their baskets with flowers, they called out for her, "Persephone, come and see what we have picked for you." And when she did not answer, they filled the mountains with their frantic shouts.

Ceres, who had just returned to Enna, was startled to hear the panic-stricken cries. She feared for her daughter and called out at once, "Where are you, my daughter?" Distraught and frantic, the goddess Ceres groaned out loud and raced at full speed, starting from the plains of Enna. As she ran, she called out either "Persephone" or "Daughter." She shouted these names again and again. But Persephone did not hear Ceres' voice, nor did Ceres hear Persephone's shouts.

When Ceres spotted a shepherd or farmer, she asked the same question, "Have you seen a young girl pass this way?" Now all the fields and meadows appear the same somber color, and a dark shadow covers the world. Now the watchdogs are silent. Ceres searched on fiery Mt. Aetna, where the ground glows red from the volcano. Here the goddess lit two pine trees to serve as torches, as she searched the world wide. She harnessed serpents to pull her chariot across the sky and she roamed the surface of the sea. She flew over Athens, crossed the Aegean, and skimmed the Ionian Sea. She passed through all the cities of Asia following a weaving erratic course. There was no place on the earth that Ceres did not visit looking for Persephone.

She mourned a very long time, and grief showed on her face. Finally Ceres approached Jupiter. "If you remember, she is your daughter; you should be concerned as well. I alone have wandered the world and have at last learned of her abduction. Dis now enjoys the reward of his crime. Persephone must not have a rapist as a husband. We cannot honor him as a son-in-law."

Jupiter tried to comfort her by saying that Dis truly loved her daughter. "But if your mind is set and you are resolved to break up this union, then let's try. We, however, can only succeed if she has fasted; if not, she will be the wife of Dis forever." The messenger god Mercury got his orders and put on his wings. He flew to the Dark Realm, but returned shortly to report that the ravished girl had eaten only three seeds of the pomegranate.

Sadly Ceres mourned again, as she had done the day her daughter was taken. "Heaven is no place for me either. I will join my daughter in the Dark Realm as well." It would have happened, but Jupiter interceded and promised that Persephone should remain above ground for twice three months. Only then was Ceres happy. She placed a crown made of grain on her head. The once fallow fields yielded an abundant harvest that year; the threshing floor could barely hold all the sheaves of grain. White is the color appropriate for Ceres. Wear white garments at Ceres' festival. No one wears dull-colored clothes.

This myth of Ceres and Persephone is driven by the agricultural cycle and the crises brought on by seasonal changes in fall with the transition between the growing time and the dormant, dead time. Persephone herself represents the seeds, for as the goddess descends to the underworld in the fall, the seeds are either placed in underground storage bins or planted in the earth at fall sowing. In the myth, she like the seed remains underground, dormant and awaiting the spring resurgence. In the classical world, greater emphasis was placed upon the loss and separation of the divine mother and daughter in September than the period of resurrection in the spring.

This loss and eventual recognition of the natural cycle serves as the nature-bound lesson of September. The rites to Ceres in September, the Eleusinian Mysteries and the Thesmophoria, had three themes: separation and loss, mourning and searching, and joy and belief. Days were set aside to ritually celebrate each of these aspects. Few other rites were practiced on the scale of these in September.

This time of year, when the growing season is finished and the dark and barren time is fast approaching, may stir up thoughts and fears inside each of us as well. September is the time to face the dark and frightening thoughts of separation from those we love. We can do this through prayer, offering, and ritual. This tale from prehistoric times touches us deeply today, for nothing is more tragic than the loss of an innocent child. The myth guides us through the stages of loss, mourning, and the final period of resolution and closure. This is the process common to all endings, all separations that we today may experience in various ways, for example, the death of a loved one, the termination of a heartfelt relationship, or the separation from home, family, or livelihood. Although we cannot avoid the pain of such life-jarring events, we are reminded that this too is part of a cycle. From the myth, we learn to deal with endings, separation, and loss of innocence. Most important, however, we are given hope for a closure and renewal. In September, we learn from Ceres and Persephone how to "harvest life."

RITES AND RITUALS OF SEPTEMBER

Separation and Loss

The loss of the daughter to the mother, the mother to the daughter, is the essential female tragedy. . . . Each daughter, even in the millennia before Christ, must have longed for a mother whose love for her and whose power were so great as to undo rape and bring her back from death. And every mother must have longed for the power of Demeter, the efficacy of her anger, the reconciliation with her lost self. (Rich, 237–40)

MODERN RITUAL OF LOSS AND SEPARATION

The myth of Ceres and Persephone is powerful and poignant. The millennia have not weakened its impact. By reading this ancient tale, you too can grieve with the goddesses.

Revisit the myth perhaps in a poetic version; reread it, reenact it, and meditate quietly on the passages. We will always experience loss and, for some of us, varying levels of depression. It cannot be denied that bad things do happen to innocent people. The myth of Ceres and Persephone reminds us that this is a process, a natural cycle, and not an end.

September 5–19, NONES–XII KALENDS OCTOBER

JUPITER

LUDI ROMANI

The Ludi Romani were the oldest and most famous games, held in honor of Jupiter Optimus Maximus.

September 13, IDES

JUPITER, JUNO, AND MINERVA

On this day in 509 B.C.E., the temple to Jupiter Optimus Maximus was dedicated. A feast was held that day and repeated in subsequent years to honor Jupiter, Juno, and Minerva. The sacred feast, or *epulum*, followed a sacrifice. Statues of the three honored deities were brought out of the temple dressed for a feast and carried to the banquet. Jupiter always reclined on a couch, while the goddesses sat in chairs. Tables laden with food and wine were placed before them while music played in the background. All the senators gathered for the banquet, making an impressive showing.

It is difficult for many of us today to imagine thousands of initiates, both male and female, slave and free, traveling weeks or even months, bearing the hardships of a lengthy and costly land or sea voyage, journeying from all over the Mediterranean world to pay homage to an exclusively female relationship, that of Demeter and her dear daughter Persephone. And it is beyond our experience to have a state-supported holiday during which for nearly two weeks all work and business yielded to the celebration of the Divine Feminine. Yet that is exactly what happened, and we lament the loss!

Mid-September

CERES AND PERSEPHONE

ELEUSINIAN MYSTERIES

The Eleusinian Mysteries were open to all persons who spoke Greek and had not committed murder. The goddesses welcomed both men and women, slave or free. The one requirement that may have prohibited participation was the fee of 15 drachmas, equivalent to about ten days' workman's wages by the fourth century B.C.E. The Greater Eleusinian Rites began in the last half of September and lasted about ten days.

Day 1: Young men selected for their physical dexterity and athleticism left Athens for the town of Eleusis to escort the sacred objects back to Athens on the following day.

Day 3: Thousands of men and women gathered in the grand Agora of Athens to declare themselves participants and hear the high priest state the rules.

Day 4: The initiates marched to the sea to purify themselves in the briny water. Each initiate also washed a piglet that he or she would sacrifice later that day.

Day 5: A sacrifice was offered to the two goddesses.

Day 7: The initiates walked along the Sacred Way to Eleusis, following behind the sacred objects. As they walked, they swung branches of myrtle tied with wool in rhythm to a beat and shouted the sacred name "Iakchos." They carried torches, as the goddess Ceres did in her search. A ritual bath in the river ended the day's journey.

The initiates were welcomed into Eleusis and, at the sight of the first star, broke their two-day fast just as the goddess had done. Special round pottery dishes and tiny cups of grain, peas, and beans were displayed for all to see. That night, the women apparently danced suggestively and sang obscene songs, although celibacy was mandatory.

Day 8: The final phase of initiation occurred in a building built solely for this purpose. The Telesterion was a large flat-roofed, windowless square hall capable of holding thousands of people on rows of seats lining the sides. In the center was the Anaktoron, a sacred stone construction, closed to view, containing the throne of the high priest. This must have been a very dark and mysterious place. The initiates drank the sacred drink, kykeon, and attended the mystery rites.

Day 9: There was dancing, feasting, and singing after the rites were completed. As a closure ceremony, a libation was made with all participants facing the east, looking to the sky, and shouting "Rain," then turning to the west, facing down at the earth, and shouting "Conceive" (or "Hye," then "Kye" in Greek). The clothes the initiates wore were later used as swaddling clothes for newborn infants.

How can a story from thousands of years ago, a myth involving the gods and goddesses probably originating in the Neolithic times, hold any meaning for us today? We all experience loss of some degree, yet coming to terms with a separation or ending takes time and can be a very slow, painful, and personal process. At some point in our lives, a ritual for loss may be appropriate and bring comfort and healing.

MODERN RITUAL:
A DANCE OF LAMENTATION AND LOSS

During times of mourning, the Naenia, or lamentation song, was traditionally sung to the accompaniment of a single flute. It was similar to a chant with several phrases repeated over and over again. Naenia, also the Goddess of Funerary

Lamentations, had a little temple near one of the gates leading into Rome. Dance, considered an invention of the goddess, had a place in many religious festivals from joyous occasions to times of mourning. The Etruscans especially danced at their funerals. A dance of mourning featured women and men moving to music and song in a slow procession. As they moved, they showed the gesture of mourning, a hand held before the face or touching the forehead.

- Choose some slow, thoughtful music that holds meaning for you.
- Choreograph a dance of loss, mourning, and searching. Your movements do not have to be elaborate, but should be heartfelt. They can be planned and danced in a group, yet this can also be a private dance performed alone.

We share something in common with those who lived two or three millennia ago—we all experience loss. Different cultures, different religions, different eras all reflect a diversity of responses to loss. A reenactment of the myth of Ceres and Persephone by participation in the ritual of the Eleusinian Mysteries provoked a personal encounter with the goddesses, who offered hope, faith, and strength to the ancient Greeks and Romans. The ancients looked to the power and mystery of the Divine Feminine for comfort and guidance through loss and the somber days of September.

MODERN RITUAL:
A LIBATION TO THE DEAD

The Romans honored their dead and those spirits who dwell underground by making a libation, an offering that the earth drinks. Often, a permanent libation hole was dug into the ground near family tombs to serve as a gateway to the dead spirits. The family would then make libation, using wine, or honey throughout the year to deceased relatives.

- Find a secluded quiet place and pour a libation into the Mother Earth as you remember those who have gone before, those you have loved.

Mourning and Searching

We humans are bound to the earth in the natural cycle of life and death, really no different than the plants and animals—something that we easily forget, but can never avoid—for the dead return to the earth and the womb of the Mother. And we search for answers and reasons. For the initiates, the September rites of Ceres and Persephone described a ritualized time of mourning and searching.

We can never know what exactly the thousands of initiates in the September rites were seeking or what they experienced with days of fasting, a demanding fourteen-mile walk, purifications, fatigue, fear, and anticipation of the unknown. We can be assured that every man and woman was personally committed to experiencing the ritual, which involved physical and emotional hardship and demanded spiritual courage. This was a quest, a search into the deeper mysteries of the inner self.

Our knowledge is scant and suspect, since few have spoken of what actually occurred in the Telesterion, the building that housed the rites. Clement of Alexandria, a Christian and initiate, tells us, "I fasted, I drank the *kykeon,* I worked, and deposited in the basket and from the basket into the chest" (*Protreptikos* 2.21.2). Kykeon was a drink of barley, water, and herbs that some suggest contained traces of barley mold (ergot), a substance similar to LSD.

We can infer, however, that a visionary state was induced from days of fasting and little food followed by a fermented beverage. But just what vision did the initiates behold? Did they find what they were seeking? The grieving and searching process was an integral part of the weeklong rite, and this experience marked a profound transformation in the lives of many men and women.

KYKEON—A MAGIC POTION DRUNK BY THE INITIATES AT THE ELEUSINIAN MYSTERIES

This magic potion prepared for thousands of years in Greece was ingested by the inititates at the Eleusinian Mysteries. This thick soup-like drink was also prepared for the heroes of the Trojan War.

"Fair-haired Hecamede made kykeon for them . . . First she moved a table up to them, a fine polished table with a dark gleaming stand: on it she placed a bronze disk with an onion in it as a relish to the drink, and also yellow honey. Next came the heap of holy barley meal. Thus, in a cup, the lovely women made a kykeon for them with Pramnian wine: she grated goat's cheese into it with a bronze grater, and sprinkled barley on it, and when she had prepared the kykeon, she invited them to drink. (Homer *Iliad* 2.638–41 Dalby 40)

A MODERN VERSION OF KYKEON *(serves four)*
(Adapted from Cato De Agricultura *85)*

²/₃ cup semolina

16 ounces ricotta cheese

¹/₃ cup honey

¹/₂ cup beaten egg

Place the semolina in a medium-sized pan, cover with water, and soak for fifteen minutes. Drain the water from the semolina and add the ricotta cheese, honey, and beaten egg. Bring slowly to a very low boil and allow to simmer for a few minutes. Cool before serving.

September/October

CERES AND PERSEPHONE
THESMOPHORIA

This rite to Ceres and Persephone was held in late September or early October and was not restricted to Greece, where it lasted three days, but was practiced in cities around the Mediterranean. In southern Italy and Sicily the ritual could last up to ten days. There, "older women respected for their noble birth and character" served as priestesses.

The Thesmophoria differs from other rites in that it is practiced only by women, young and old, mothers and daughters, "maidens and matrons." Here, too, the myth of Ceres and Persephone lies at the core of the ritual. The three aspects of the myth, the separation, the mourning and search, and the joyful reunion, were reenacted and collectively experienced by women in antiquity.

175

In preparation for the ritual, one month in advance, the priestess of the Thesmophoria threw live pigs into a sacrificial pit. On the first day of the rite, the women made a procession to a building or specially constructed huts at the outskirts of the town where they would live for the duration of the ritual. They refrained from wearing crowns of flowers on their heads as Persephone was collecting flowers when she was abducted. The women carried with them closed baskets—what they contained we don't know, perhaps clay phalluses or sheaves of grain. Later this day, they would open the pit, and a priestess would descend and bring up the rotted remains of the pigs to be placed upon an altar.

This unusual ritual of resurrection of the dead from underground began a period of mourning that lasted through the second day. The women remained secluded, fasting and sleeping on freshly cut green boughs and branches. On the second night, they would run through the streets with torches, stopping at crossroads to shout, reenacting Ceres' frantic search for Persephone.

The third day, or last phase, was festive with special meals, singing, and dancing. Though sexual abstinence was mandatory, sexual symbolism predominated. Phallic-shaped cakes were baked and eaten. Obscene gestures, songs, and dances were encouraged, to the great delight of the men passing by. Blood-colored objects, such as red wine and red pomegranates, were part of the ritual. In honor of Persephone, however, the pomegranates were not eaten. When all was over, the women returned home to be united with their families, as Ceres was with Persephone.

In September, we now look to the end, to a time when "Now all the fields and meadows appear the same somber color, and a dark shadow covers the world. Now the watchdogs are silent . . ."—a time of closure, withdrawal, and death. The goddesses guide us with burning torches, for the two gifts that Ceres gives to humans are the grain harvested in the fall and the mystery rituals.

MODERN RITUAL FOR A PERSONAL LOSS

I once joined a group of women celebrating the September ritual at a mountain retreat. At night, when all was dark, we lit a huge bonfire, read the myth of Ceres and Persephone, and then shared some painful moments of loss, separation, abuse, and denial. Then, carefully, we each took a lit branch or candle and wandered off alone for a short distance down darkened paths as we searched within ourselves, to grieve and to meditate upon our own personal losses.

Joy and Belief

Much as Easter confirms the resurrection of Christ for Christians and revolves around the sacred story of a divine Parent and Child, the September rituals to Ceres confirmed the cycle of life, death, and rebirth to ancient pagans. Yet, contrary to the Christian version of the divine Father and Son, the pagan story was based upon the Holy Mother and Daughter, the principle of the Divine Feminine.

The great Roman statesman Cicero, as an initiate into the September Eleusinian rites, had a very personal encounter with the goddess Ceres and her daughter. He confessed this profound and intimate moment of self-enlightenment in a letter to his friend Atticus: "We have come to truly understand the first principles of life, and we have accepted with joy not only a rationale for living, but even for dying with better hope" (*De Legibus* 2.36). We all seek happiness on earth and blessedness after death. How powerful it must have been to hear the myth retold, to actually reenact it and participate in the cycle within a spiritual community, and to take partake in the mystery. September challenges us to face endings; it is a month of separation. September also conditions a belief in the sanctity of nature, the Divine Feminine, and the continuous natural cycle of all things. And it gives us hope for what will come as we do what we are compelled to do, "harvest life."

AN ANCIENT PRAYER FOR THE SEEDS

O grant unto the tender seedlings unbroken increase,
Let not the sprouting shoot be nipped by chilly snows.
When we sow, let the sky be cloudless and winds blow fair;
But when the seed is buried then sprinkle it with water from the sky.
Forbid the birds—pests of the tilled land—to devastate the fields of grain
    with their destructive flocks.
You too, ants, spare the sown grain; so shall you have a more abundant harvest.
Meantime may no disease blight the growing crop nor foul weather turn it a
    sickly hue;
May it neither shrivel up nor swell unduly and be choked.
May the fields be free blight and no barren oats spring from the tilled soil.
May the farm yield many times crops of wheat, barley and grain which can
    be baked.
May the Two Goddess grant our prayers.
Long time did wars engage mankind and the plow gave way to the sword.
    The plow ox gave way to the war horse.
Hoes were idle, a helmet was made out of a heavy rake.
Thanks be to the Goddesses and to my house.
Let War be laid in chains.
Yoke now the oxen and sow the seed in the ploughed earth.
Peace is the nurse of Ceres and Ceres is the Child of Peace! (Ovid Fasti
    1.679–704 LCL)

OCTOBER

THE MONTH TO PROMISE

ISIS, MISTRESS OF THE HOUSE OF LIFE

I, the natural mother of all life, the mistress of the elements, the first child of time, the supreme divinity, the queen of those in hell, the first among those in heaven, the uniform manifestation of all the gods and goddesses—

I, who govern by my nod the crests of light in the sky, the purifying wafts of the ocean, and the lamentable silences of hell—

I, whose single godhead is venerated all over the earth under manifold forms, varying rites, and changing names— (Apuleius Golden Ass 11.5, Lindsey)

Rural Menologia
SUN IN LIBRA
31 DAYS
NONES: OCTOBER 7
DAYLIGHT: 10³⁄₄ HOURS
DARKNESS: 13³⁄₄ HOURS

→>•<←

Ancient farmers were advised to pick the grapes and press the new wine at the vindemia, the vintage. (Menologia)

◎◎◎◎◎

Nine months have passed since we began our journey, pacing the agricultural cycle month by month from the times of new growth to maturity and eventual harvest. We now arrive at October, the month of the fall vintage, when the plump juicy grapes that have ripened on the vine during languid summer days are finally plucked and pressed, producing a frothy deep purple new wine. Now the dappled sunlight is noticeably shorter and the cold dark time of winter rapidly approaches. Life in the natural world this month goes underground as animals hunker down for the long haul, birds retreat to warmer climates, and seeds lie dormant awaiting the period of rebirth. We also beat a hasty retreat into the dry, warm confines of home and hearth, driven inside by chilling temperatures and drenching rains. In some regions, an icy crystal blanket covers the fields and trees at the first frost. October portends the bleak winter season, while nature herself compels us to consider endings and death.

In ancient Roman times, October marked an end to an intensely active period for farming as well as travel, commerce, and military conquest. During this fall month, farmers busily prepared for the coming of winter, making certain of adequate supplies and provisions to last through the dark cold months looming just ahead. Likewise, the threat of snow and treacherous weather brought a halt to much of the travel and trade in the ancient world. In fact, in the earliest days of Rome, military campaigns lasted from March through October, when the Roman soldiers returned to their homes and farms. October was the month when many activities came to an abrupt end. Appropriately, the Isia, the sacred rites to the goddess Isis and her days of mourning for her lost husband, Osiris, were held in ancient Rome during the final days of this month.

Isis was originally an Egyptian goddess worshiped by the people living along the Nile River since prehistoric times. During the second and first centuries B.C.E., however, her cult spread throughout the Mediterranean, reaching Italy, where her popularity grew among Romans of all classes from members of the imperial family to slaves. Her fall ritual, the Isia, which ran from October 28 to November 3, became so popular in the Roman world that it was added to the rustic Roman calendar, the rural menologia, about 40 C.E. Who was this most ancient Egyptian goddess? What does Queen Isis offer?

In the beginning was Isis, Oldest of the Old, Great Lady of Egypt, Queen of Heaven and Mistress of the House of Life, represented by the ankh, her symbol for "life." In antiquity, this goddess found faithful worshipers among people of all social rank dwelling in such far-flung lands as Egypt, Ethiopia, Greece, Italy, Spain, Germany, Britain, and the shores of the Arabian Gulf and Black Sea. The goddess Isis welcomed all and did not discriminate by gender, social class, wealth, or racial background. Isis bestowed her love on all peoples and was a goddess of redemption and forgiveness, welcoming those who had sinned equally with the sinless. Isis gave freely of love, pity, compassion, and forgiveness, for she herself had known great sorrow. Isis, the Mother of Life, offered unconditional love.

The worship of Isis brought hope and meaning to many people, as she addressed directly the eternal questions of life and death. Queen Isis sails her sacred ship on a journey to the very borders of the world of the dead. And she returns. Thus, it is also fitting that the Isia was held in late October, a focused period of endings and closure, when the worlds of the living and dead touched and the veil between them was thin. Today we experience this dark magical time as Halloween, All Hallows' Eve, Samhain, or the Day of the Dead. In antiquity, these days of October belonged to Queen Isis.

The story of Isis is a very old one and has been retold and reshaped over thousands of years by people of many different cultures living in countries throughout the Mediterranean world. This myth of a dying god, a grieving goddess, and a sacred birth is rooted in the natural cycle of the Nile River and the yearly ebb and flow of its life-sustaining waters. It is ultimately a story of faith, hope, and love.

Isis and Osiris

Geb, the Great God of Earth, and Nut, the Supreme Goddess of the Sky, produced their first offspring, Isis and Osiris, who, while still in their mother's womb, had fallen in love and mated. Isis and her brother/husband, Osiris, formed a perfect union and ruled the world in peace.

Osiris traveled across the lands bearing gifts to all people. It was Osiris who sent forth the sun's rays to all parts of the world both on land and sea.

Osiris evoked anger and jealously in his brother, Seth, who plotted revenge. Seth attacked Osiris and treacherously murdered him.

Isis deeply mourned the loss of her brother/husband, Osiris, traveling the land for many days in search of his body, when she learned that Seth had savagely dismembered the corpse and scattered the parts in various places. She grieved and mourned his loss openly. The unconstrained flood of tears down her divine cheeks fell gently into the Nile River, causing the annual inundation so essential for the continuity of all life forms, vegetal, animal, and human. Divine Isis found and retrieved all the parts of her beloved except the phallus. She miraculously mated with the dead Osiris, conceiving the child Horus in a union with her dead husband. Osiris was brought back to life by the magic of Isis, who breathed the wind of life into his nostrils. Osiris was reborn and resurrected in the image of his own posthumous son Horus. Thus, the great god Osiris was reborn through the child Horus and continued the struggle with the evil Seth, finally vanquishing his powerful enemy and rising to rule the world once again.

It was the wish of Isis that all people living in Egypt honor Osiris. So she made out of spices and wax many replicas of the body of Osiris. The goddess then called together all the priests from all the regions of Egypt and instructed them to take a waxen image of Osiris back to their various districts and bury it with the rites of mourning. Isis told the priests to worship Osiris as a great god and at the same time to sanctify an animal native to each of their districts. Therefore, each region in Egypt claimed to possess the tomb of Osiris and venerated a variety of animals held sacred to the god.

We learn from this story about endings and death; we learn of faith and commitment; and we come to understand the promise of salvation. The goddess Isis teaches the capacity to feel deeply and to express outwardly the pain brought on by immeasurable grief. We learn to face those difficult moments in our lives when we become separated from our loved ones or when we face the conclusion or ending of something special such as a job, a project, or a relationship. We learn that the aging process and death itself are integral components of the natural cycle. Together, we can grieve with this goddess, knowing that she understands: "Isis cries out with a loud voice and the earth quakes" (*Pyramid Texts* 1270).

From Isis we also learn forgiveness and acceptance and to cherish those close to us. Isis offers the blessings of faith, hope, and love. Isis teaches us to honor the earth and respect all forms of animal life, for they are manifestations of the divine. The powers of Isis, too, are rooted within the natural world. Her tears over Osiris initiated the yearly inundation of the Nile's water, so vital to all life in Egypt. Isis was the soil of Egypt commingling with the Nile waters to bring fertility. As Life-Giver, Isis was the goddess of all animals, yet the cat, held sacred in ancient Egypt, was special to her. Her cult creatures also included the cow, falcon, vulture, ibis, crocodile, gazelle, goose, and swallow. On her head she wore the crown of her sacred snake, the asp. Cleopatra, who envisioned herself as the goddess Isis incarnate, chose to die by the bite of the asp.

The many components of the natural world are each sacred, entwined, and interrelated—the seed, the tree, the animal that feeds from the tree, human that feeds from the tree and the animal. Each goes through similar phases of life—birth, growth, death, and return to the eternal womb (the earth), an endless cycle of rebirth and renewal. For those who believe devoutly in the goddess Isis, nature may be manifest in the various gods and goddesses, but in essence they are really only One. By whatever path you take, whatever name you invoke, whatever rite you perform, you honor the One Divine Feminine.

> *The ancient Greeks called me Minerva; those living on the island of Cyprus worship me as Venus; the people of Crete hail me as Diana; the Sicilians call me the ancient goddess Ceres. Some call me Juno; some call me Hecate; some Ramnusia or Bellona. Yet those who are enlightened by the earliest rays of the divine sun, those who exceed all others in ancient lore and worship me by the customs of their ancestors, the Egyptians call me Queen Isis. (Apuleius Golden Ass 11.5)*

RITES AND RITUALS OF OCTOBER

Endings and Death

October marked the end of the growing cycle, now completed with the harvesting of the grapes and the making of wine. It was vintage time for ancient Roman farmers, time to clean and fumigate the wine cellar. Early October was a busy time as the farmers gathered in the olives and bunches of ripe grapes. The grapes were then mounded in large batches on special pressing floors in the rural villas, where the pressed juice was then stored in large holding vessels called *doliae* as next year's wine.

MODERN RITUAL TO EXPERIENCE NATURE AND ONENESS

Find a secluded place outside to meditate on a quiet October day, perhaps the sacred spot in your garden or a special retreat known only to you. Let all of your senses take in the beauty of nature. Think deeply on these thoughts as the Buddhist monk Thich Nhat Hanh teaches us to honor this feeling of oneness and connection with nature and the divine:

> Contemplate a leaf, with its rich red or golden color as it hangs on the branch ready to fall to the ground at the slightest breeze. Consider that the leaf had been a mother to the tree. During the spring and summer, the leaf had worked to nourish the tree. Yet when it falls to the ground, as it must, and returns to the soil of Mother Earth, it continues to nourish the tree. Be comforted in the knowledge the dying leaf will again return to the branch of the tree, soon, next spring. (116–17)

October 1, KALENDS

FIDES

The goddess Fides, or "Good Faith," was honored on this day in ancient Rome. Before offering sacrifice, the priests wrapped their hands as far as their fingers with a cloth in a gesture symbolizing that faith must be kept.

Fides represented the relationship between deity and humankind, not faith between people. This day marked a commitment to one's faith relationship with the divine. It was said that the statue of Fides had her right hand bound in a gesture of faith-keeping.

This was also the end of the campaigning season for the Roman army in the earliest days of the city. The soldiers put away their weapons and prepared for the cold dark winter months, approaching so quickly now. The rite of the October Horse and the Armilustrium celebrated the closure of the warring season.

October 5, III NONES

MUNDUS OPENED

The door to the Underworld, the *mundus*, was opened for the second time in the year. (See August 24.)

JUPITER AND BACCHUS

MEDITRINALIA

The name of the festival, Meditrinalia, comes from the word meaning "to be healed," because in oldest times this was the day to pour an offering of new and old wine and to taste it in order to be healed. It was appropriate to repeat a phrase such as "Wine new and old I drink, of illness new and old I am cured." The toast made on this day was to either Jupiter or Bacchus.

October 13, III IDES

FONS

FONTINALIA

Fons, the God of Springs, was honored this day, when garlands were thrown into springs or placed on the tops of wells. Today we throw coins.

October 15, IDES

MARS

OCTOBER HORSE

On this day a two-horse chariot race occurred in the Field of Mars in Rome. The horse on the right side of the winning team was sacrificed to Mars in a grisly ritual with both military and agricultural implications.

October 19, XIV KALENDS NOVEMBER

MARS

ARMILUSTRIUM

This was a day to honor Mars and to purify the soldiers polluted by bloodshed over the summer months.

As the days of October pass, we too are driven by the natural world to face the dwindling sunlight and conclusion of the growing season. Nature gives final notice in many regions where the forested hillsides glow with striking fall colors of the turning leaves, the brilliant golds, the vibrant reds and oranges—marking an end, a closure to the period of green growth. It seems as though the end is upon us with the bare trees and brown countryside, and we await the barren months.

October is a magical time, when the two worlds of the living and the dead overlap, and we are forced to deal directly with death. It is a time of emptiness, when dark spirits roam the earth striking fear into our very souls. This is the month of Halloween and the Day of the Dead, when it is the custom to visit the cemetery to honor those departed. Just as Isis faced the death of her beloved Osiris, she gives us the courage and focus to face death and endings. Expressing grief and sadness with Isis is part of the spiritual process.

MODERN RITUAL TO HONOR DEPARTED ONES

The final solemn days of October provide an opportunity to reconnect with those who have gone before. We already celebrate Halloween with images of ghosts, goblins, and skeletons connoting the season of death and endings. This is also the time to visit the graves of one's ancestors and bear flowers or small offerings to the dead spirits.

October is the time to think of the beloved dead. Visit the cemetery if possible to honor the graves of those departed. Alternatively, find a quiet place outside, close to the earth, and meditate for a few minutes upon those dear ones who have died; think over each loss experienced this past year whether from death or separation. Allow the tears to come and gently comfort yourself with warm memories of fond times. Learn to express sadness and grief! Remember it was the tears of Isis that started the annual life-giving Nile floods.

In Sicily, legend has it that the dead leave their tombs during these days, raiding the best pastry shops to bring children special treats such as these Dead Man's Cookies.

DEAD MAN'S COOKIES *(makes about 5 dozen)*

These cookies are eaten in Italy on All Soul's Day, when they are shaped to look like fava beans, a symbol of the dead in ancient Rome. Recall the May ritual to the dead spirits, the Lemuria, where beans were used to propitiate the dead.

"The grappa [an Italian brandy] in this Venetian sweet gives the cookies a distinct and slightly bitter edge. The same cookies are made in Rome without pine nuts or grappa by reducing the almonds to a fine powder, adding at tiny bit more butter, and flavoring them with cinnamon."

1 1/2 to 1 3/4 cups blanched almonds	grated zest of 1 lemon
1/2 cup sugar	1 tablespoon butter
1/4 cup unbleached all-purpose flour	1 egg
1 1/2 tablespoons pine nuts, coarsely chopped	1 egg yolk
1 tablespoon grappa	1 egg white for glaze

In a food processor fitted with the steel blade or with a sharp knife, chop the almonds into fine grains, but not a powder. Move them to the bowl of an electric mixer or to a large mixing bowl and add the sugar, flour, pine nuts, grappa, lemon zest, butter, egg, and egg yolk. Mix on the lowest speed in the electric mixer or stir together by hand. The dough initially seems very dry, but does eventually smooth out and come together. If you are really having trouble, add egg white, a teaspoon at a time.

Butter and flour baking sheets or line them with parchment paper. Divide the dough into several pieces. On a lightly floured work surface roll each one into a long narrow log about 3/4 inch wide. Cut into 1-inch segments, about the size of a fava bean. Roll each one slightly to smooth out the edges, then press a small indentation in the center, so that the cookies really do resemble the fava beans. Set on the baking sheets. Whip the egg white until it is frothy and brush a little bit on each cookie.

Bake cookies at 300 degrees until pale gold in color, 20 to 25 minutes. Cool on racks. (Field, 229)

Faith and Commitment

The unsettling time of October, the period of death and separation, can be bridged. Hope can be kindled during this somber dark time. Yet, faith and belief in the divine are required, and spiritual commitment is critical. For Apuleius, a Roman author of the second century C.E., and for many Romans, true belief was in the divine goddess Isis. With her, there was no dark abyss, no empty void.

October 28–November 3, VII KALENDS–II NONES NOVEMBER

I S I S

ISIA

Since the worship of Isis was another mystery religion, very little is known of the events of the Isia. The procession to her shrine, however, was a mesmerizing event. The parade began with men and women dressed "as their votive fancy desired" leading the way. A chorus of women followed wearing only white and strewing the path with flower blossoms and perfumed oils. Others came in order carrying torches and waxen candles to honor She Who Made the Stars of Heaven.

Next followed musicians and a choir of young people in snow-white garments singing songs to the pipers' tune. Then came the priests and priestess shouting, "Make way for the goddess." A band of men and women of all classes and ages who had been initiated into the mysteries of the goddess and who wore linen clothes of the purest white followed. The women had their hair done up with veils of the finest silk covering their heads; the men had all shaven their heads. They each carried a silver or bronze sistrum, rattling the sacred instrument as they walked.

Isis was accessible to slave and emperor alike and could be approached through personal prayer. She listened to all supplications and required only faith and devotion from her followers, not money or expensive offerings. Two thousand years ago, Apuleius invoked her presence with devout faith as follows:

Queen of Heaven, who wanders through many sacred groves, and who is worshiped and esteemed in different ways, O, Goddess of the Moon who shines upon the walls of cities with beams of female light, who nurtures the seeds in the earth with your moist heat, and glows with divine radiance when the sun has set. O by whatever name, and by whatever rites, and in whatever form that you may be invoked, come now and help me in my hour of need. And, moved by the prayer and declaration of faith, she appeared:

The first thing that I noticed was her abundant dark hair falling gently in soft curls onto her neck. Upon her head, she wore a garland woven with a great variety of flowers. She was crowned with a divine tiara worthy of description, for in the center, just above her forehead, was a plain circular object that was in fact a miniature full moon that glowed with a soft clear white light. On either side of the moonlike globe, two serpents were placed together with sheaves of grain.

Her multicolored gown was of the finest linen, a part was pure white, another was dyed the color of yellow crocuses, with a third the color of rich red roses. Yet, the pitch-black cloak around her shoulders caught my eye, for it shone with a dark glow. This amazing garment fell in soft folds of fabric, swaying gracefully to the ground in a hem of knotted fringe. The elaborate border seemed to cling to the garment of its own accord, of brilliant hues, comprising every kind of fruit and flower. This magical cloak was sprinkled with glowing stars and in the center was a full moon emitting soft moon beams in every direction. The goddess held in her right hand a bronze rattle, a sistrum, her sacred instrument. She carried a miniature golden boat in her left. An asp with raised head and puffed out throat encircled her right arm. Such was the goddess Isis. (Apuleius *Golden Ass* 11.5)

MODERN RITUAL OF AFFIRMATION

Take some time to examine your faith and your spirituality as October draws us on toward the darkest months. Affirming your faith is a very personal act; reaffirm your faith with an appropriate ceremony or just a personal prayer. October is a good month to look seriously at your spiritual life. Visit your church, temple, or place of worship, or just head outside to a park or garden. Find someplace where you can think deeply, light a candle, or meditate privately for a little while.

Often organizations or religious centers conduct day or weekend retreats for contemplation and prayer. You may wish to recommit to your faith or consider conversion to a new form of belief. Take heart! October was the month of the goddess Fides, or Faith, and the month for commitment.

In October we come to examine our spiritual foundation and our beliefs. The cold outside, the darkened sky, the gray hues, and somber tones of the natural world seep inside of us through all our pores. The natural world won't let us escape, but prods us on to think long, heavy thoughts of death and search for a spiritual solution and solace. As much as we pretend to be so sophisticated with modern technological achievements, we really are no different than the ancient Romans living two thousand years ago—those pagans faced the same questions we do regarding birth, life, and death. They likewise sought personal answers in the spiritual world.

MODERN RITUAL: PRAYER OF AFFIRMATION

When praying to the deities, the Romans spoke the words outside in the open air in the privacy of a garden or in a temple precinct. The customary way to pray was with palms facing upward and outstretched hands. Read aloud this marvelous prayer to the divine:

Most holy and everlasting Redeemer of the human race, you kindly cherish our lives and bestow the consoling smiles of a mother upon our hardships. There is no day or night, not a moment in time, that is not filled with the eternity of your mercy.

You protect us on land or sea. You chase away the storms of life and stretch out your hand to help the dejected and troubled. You can untangle the hopelessly entwined threads of the Fates. You can mitigate the tempests of Fortune, and check the stars bent on an unfortunate course. The gods of heaven worship you. The gods of hell bow before you. You rotate the globe. You light the sun. You govern space. You trample hell. The stars move to your orders. The seasons return, the gods rejoice, the elements combine. At your nod, the breezes blow, clouds collect, seeds sprout, blossoms increase. The birds that fly in the air, the beasts that roam on the hills, the serpents that hide in the earth, the fishes that swim in the ocean tremble before your Majesty.

My voice has no power to utter what I think of you. Not a thousand mouths with a thousand tongues, not an eternal flow of unwearied declaration could give you sufficient praises. Poor as I am, I shall do all that a truly religious person can do. I will hold your divine countenance within my breast, and there in the secret depths I shall keep divinity for ever guarded. (Apuleius *Golden Ass* 11.5, Lindsey)

Promise and Salvation

Isis was creatrix, protectress, healer, and deliverer from suffering. She also offered the promise and hope of rebirth and rejuvenation, and this seems to be at the core of her rituals. Initiation into the cult of Isis in antiquity was a mysterious process, and we know very little since the steps to conversion were private and guarded, rarely spoken about, just as the Eleusinian rites to Ceres were. Apuleius does give us a glimmer of the magic moment in which he was reborn: "I underwent a near death experience as I descended to the underworld ruled by Persephone. Yet I returned. It was midnight, yet I saw the sun shining in all of its majesty. I touched the gods below and the gods above. I stood next to them. I worshiped them.... I was born again" (Apuleius *Golden Ass* 11.23, Lindsey).

Indeed, this is a very powerful statement describing a very personal moment of enlightenment and union with the divine. Isis promised rebirth and salvation to those who believed. During the Isia, on a special day called the "Finding of Osiris," worshipers reenacted the myth of Isis and Osiris, sharing the grief and the joy of Isis searching for the body of Osiris and finally finding it and embalming it. They shouted in unison, *"Heurekamen, synchairomen,"* "We have found! We rejoice together!" It is also said that in one rite during the Isia worshipers gathered in a darkened room and mourned over a prone statue of Osiris. During the ritual, a light was carried into the room; a priest then anointed the throats of the mourners with oil and whispered, "Take heart, O Initiates, for the god is saved, and we shall have salvation" (Firmicus Maternus, *The Error of Pagan Religions* 22.1).

Hope and salvation from all of our troubles and suffering, overcoming our fear of death, and living a blessed life on earth are promises that resonate in all religions throughout the ages. These words of Isis can find meaning for each of us especially during the dark and doubt-filled days of October, when the end of the year and darkness looms in the path ahead.

MODERN RITUAL OF PROMISE AND HOPE: "THE SHIP OF ISIS"

In antiquity, a yearly ritual to Isis was carried out on a beach or near water. A model ship was prepared. It was painted with sacred words and text, bearing a special message for the year's prosperous journey. Worshipers gathered around the boat, first purifying it with flame, egg, and sulfur and chanting solemn prayers. They then piled it with small gifts, winnowing fans, perfumes, and incense and threw libations of milk mixed with grain into the water. The small ship was set adrift and allowed to sail away on its own, following its own course. Thus, the rite ended.

- Adapt this rite, adding your own very personal prayers and messages.
- Give a small offering to the goddess, remembering that she does not ask for riches or wealth, but commitment. In return she offers faith, hope, and love.
- Set your ship adrift upon the water to be guided by the goddess.

The Promise of Isis

Behold, I come to you in your time of trouble. I come with solace and aid. Put an end to your crying and tears, send your sorrows away. Soon through my benevolence will the sun of salvation rise up. Listen to what I say with great care.

You will live a blessed life. You will live a glorious life under my care and guidance. When you have traveled your full length of time and go down unto death, there also, I will be beside you. You will see me shining on amidst the darkness.

Through your religious devotion and constant faith, you may learn that I have it within my power to prolong your life beyond the limits set to it by Fate. Through me, you may be reborn. (Apuleius Golden Ass 11.5)

NOVEMBER

THE MONTH TO ACCEPT

*"Lord of the Underworld, we will return to you one day. We will come to you
eventually, for this will be our final home."* (Ovid Metamorphoses 10.34–35)

Rural Menologia

SUN IN SCORPIO

30 DAYS

NONES: NOVEMBER 5

DAYLIGHT: 9 1/4 HOURS

DARKNESS: 14 3/4 HOURS

Ancient farmers were advised to sow the fall wheat and barley and to trench around the trees. (Menologia)

November has arrived. There is a chill in the air, and the hours of sunlight are noticeably shorter. Those colder gray days of winter are on their way. Perhaps the first frost has appeared or even a light dusting of snow. The green growing season is definitely over and gone for one more year. The grains have been threshed, the apples and crops picked, the grapes pressed into new wine and stored, and the seeds placed in underground bins to keep over the winter. We have journeyed through the sensual months of spring, those months of creative energy fueled by youthful hormonal exuberance. We have passed the months of fullness and ripeness, and continued on through the harvest period of endings.

In November, Roman farmers prepared for the long, hard winter rapidly approaching, stocking up plenty of fodder and wood to keep the home warm for the cold months. On a spiritual level in the Roman calendar, with the intensity of September's and October's rituals over, everything seems to wind down in November. There is a calm in November, and we are midway through the autumn season, a good month away from the solstice and the crisis invoked by seasonal change.

The year, in many ways is a metaphor for our lives, and this is apparent as we reach these last few months. Death awaits each of us—a fact of the life cycle that we cannot change and that becomes more apparent as we age. As the dark noticeably predominates over daylight, November marks the time of acceptance and acknowledgment of the final time, the dying time. The all-encompassing bond with nature and the intimate association with the span of human life and the natural yearly cycle is evident and forms a core Roman belief in this passage by Ovid, in which the tone is acceptance:

> *What? Don't you see that the year follows in four phases, imitating our own lifetime? In early spring, it is youthful and full of new life just like a little baby; in spring all things green and growing are also young and fragile, bursting with life yet without strength, to fill the farmers with hopes of an abundant crop.*

Then, everything is in bloom and the fertile fields burst with brightly colored flowers; yet still the foliage lacks strength and endurance. After spring has passed, the year has grown more sturdy, and passes into summer. It becomes like a strong young man, full of life. There is no hardier time than this, none more full of rich warm life. Then autumn comes with its first flush of youth gone; ripe and mellow midway between youth and age, with a sprinkling of gray hair at the temples. And then comes aged winter, with faltering step and shivering, the hair all gone or frosted white. (Ovid Metamorphoses 15.200–30)

The finality and inevitability of death is eloquently expressed in this deeply moving myth of Orpheus and his most beloved Eurydice.

Orpheus and Eurydice

Hymen, the God of Marriage, wearing his saffron-colored robe traditional for weddings, made his way to the country of the Ciconian people. He was summoned by the famed singer and poet Orpheus to preside over his holy marriage to his beloved Eurydice. Yet Hymen brought with him neither joy nor good fortune. The marriage torch that he carried that day kept sputtering, filling the eyes with smoke, for it would not ignite into a flame. Instead of a blessed and happy event, the day was marred with tragedy. Eurydice, excited and nervous over the approaching nuptials, went walking in the grassy fields with her bridal attendants. A poisonous snake bit her on the ankle, killing her instantly.

Wretched Orpheus filled his days on the earth by mourning for his beloved Eurydice. He decided in desperation to try the world of the Di Manes, the Dark Shades. He dared to venture underground, passing through the portal to the World of the Dead. Summoning great courage and driven by his undying love for Eurydice, he braved the misty ghosts and spirits of those dead and buried, as he sought the realm of Hades, Lord of the Dead. He came to Persephone and Hades himself, who rules those hideous realms.

Then Orpheus took out his lyre and sang, "O Divine Ones, who rule the world that lies beneath the earth, the world to which we all who are born mortal fall back, permit me to tell the true story from my heart.

"I have not come as a threat to you or from simple curiosity. I journey to find my bride, who was killed when a snake shot poison into her body and snatched her from me in her youthful years. I have sought the strength to go on, and I have tried to bear the grief and ache of loneliness without Eurydice. I swear by this fearsome place, by this huge void, these vast and silent realms of the Underworld. I beg you to unravel the fate of my Eurydice. We pledge ourselves totally to you, though we linger on the earth a while longer. We will return to you one day. We will come to you eventually, for this will be our final home. You, Hades, rule the human race for the longest time.

"Eurydice will be yours to rule when she is old and has lived out her life. I ask the enjoyment of her days on the earth as my beloved wife. If this is denied, I am resolved not to return to the world of the living. Rejoice, Hades, then in the death of two people."

As he sang these words accompanying himself on his lyre, the bloodless spirits wept. The cheeks of the old women, the Three Fates, were wet with tears. Persephone, Queen of the Underworld, and Lord Hades could not refuse Orpheus's plaintive request. They called Eurydice, who was new among the Dark Shades. She came haltingly, limping from the wounded ankle. Orpheus greeted her with joy. Yet Hades imposed one condition—that Orpheus should not turn his eyes backward until he had left the Underworld and was again in the land of the living. If he did not abide by this condition, the gift of Eurydice's life would be in vain.

Then the husband led his dear wife, taking the sharply sloping path upward through the places of utter silence, a steep and treacherous path to follow, not well marked and shrouded in pitch-black darkness.

They came near to the entrance of the Underworld, the margin separating the Dark World from the Light, the dead from the living. Orpheus halted. Fearful that Eurydice may be afraid of the final step and so eager for a sight of her living and breathing, Orpheus turned to gaze at Eurydice with longing eyes. Instantly, she slipped backward into the depths. In panic, he stretched out his arms to grab her, to feel her solid flesh, and to save her. Sadly, he clasped nothing but the thin air.

Now, dying a second time, Eurydice did not blame her husband. What complaint could she have except that she was dearly beloved and that Orpheus had risked his life to save her. Eurydice said one last word, "Farewell," which scarcely reached her husband's ears. She fell back again to the dark and silent place she had just come from.

Orpheus was stunned by his wife's double death. He prayed and wished in vain to return to the Underworld, yet the gate was shut to him. Seven days he sat in filthy rags with no taste of food. Suffering, anguish of soul, and tears were his only nourishment. Shunning the love of all women, he wandered for years in grief and misery. One day, Orpheus came to a grove of cypress trees where he sat singing and playing his lyre. With his songs, he enthralled the wild beasts who gathered around him; he enticed the trees and commanded the stones to listen. As he sang, he was attacked by a band of wild Bacchantes and killed. The poet's shade fled quickly beneath the earth, where he recognized all the places he had seen before. Seeking the realm of the dead again, Orpheus found his beloved Eurydice and caught her in his arms. Side by side they walk together in eternity. Orpheus follows Eurydice as she leads the way. Now he may safely look upon his dear wife, his beloved Eurydice.

The gravitational pull of death and the Underworld is poignantly expressed in this myth. We learn that any struggle against or denial of it is a futile effort, and acceptance and love are essential in death and dying. Human bonds of love are not broken by death, which instead accepts all that we have and love. We learn to accept what is most painful, which is the loss of love and those whom we love. The lesson of the myth is that death does not destroy love, but instead transforms it into songs of loss or the poetry of remembrance. In the myth, love almost conquers death, as the infernal deities, Persephone and Hades, were so moved by Orpheus's song and poem that they granted the conditional return of his beloved Eurydice. With the loss of his bride a second time, Orpheus returned to this world of the living alone. Yet his love for her never died, for he expressed the passion and intensity in his poems and songs so beautiful and melancholic that they charmed the natural world—the animals, the trees, and even the stones.

We each may chose different ways at different times in our lives to deal with the death of loved ones. One way, which may be appropriate at the time, is to distance ourselves from the pain. Yet eventually we must accept the passing life and hold close within us the memory of those we loved. We can empathize with Orpheus's great suffering, which led him to face the Dark Realm and attempt to reverse the fate of his dear Eurydice. He did not succeed. He was forced to live with the pain of his twice-dead wife—a double loss and intensified grief. Eurydice accepted this knowing that she was loved. As the years passed, Orpheus learned also to accept and live with the pain, yet he never gave up his love. Instead, he honored the deep love in exquisite song and deeply moving poetry. He came to accept her mortality, for he had no other choice. In November, the period of growth and life comes to an end as the cycle of nature moves forward. In November we learn acceptance of life's final struggle. And we wait.

RITES AND RITUALS OF NOVEMBER

Acceptance

This month of November we can finally see the end drawing near. The year is moving rapidly to completion. Our period of great activity is over; we are resigned and ready for a change, something new, and the cycle to continue.

MODERN RITUAL: REMEMBERING THE DEAD

One cold and dark day in November, our women's group gathered to honor the spirits of the month and the natural cycle. Though departure and death is not easy to talk about for many of us, this was the chosen and appropriate theme for the month. This was a solemn time and not a gay and festive celebration, yet one so powerful, essential, and natural.

We came together to share memories of those whom we have loved and who have departed this life. One by one we placed a long thin black veil over our heads envisioning the fearful descent of Orpheus into the darkened underworld. Here, we shared thoughts of beloved ones, visiting again those deeply personal memories and evoking love bonds that never died.

When all was over, we said a final "Farewell" much like Eurydice. And we moved a step closer to resolution and acceptance of the death of our loved ones and to our own mortality.

November 8, VI IDES

MUNDUS OPENED

The Mundus, the door to the Underworld, was opened for the third time in the year and the dead spirits could roam the streets. (See August 24, October 5.)

The Mundus is again opened and dead spirits can roam the streets of Rome free to return home. At this time of year, with Halloween and the Day of the Dead just past, we are forced to face the ultimate fate head on. In November, we look death right in the eye, and there is no denying, no avoiding the final outcome. By dealing with the themes of loss, separation, and death so prevalent in the rituals of September, we prepare ourselves. By symbolically experiencing death and rebirth with Isis and Osiris in October we do the same. Most important, by evaluating and recommitting to our faith, we learn to accept the inevitable. In the yearly agrarian and natural cycle, November is indeed the autumn of our lives; we are growing old. These are the issues of November.

The Greeks and Romans tended to divide the years of the aging process into groups or spans, yet there was no general agreement on the length of these spans. For practical purposes it is easier to view the life span in three phases of youth, maturity, and old age, marked in women by the onset of menstruation, years of fertility, and menopause.

Menstruation was believed to occur in the fourteenth year for young girls, as their bodies were sufficiently developed to allow the collection and evacuation of blood. The first sign of puberty and the cause for a coming-of-age dedication was not menstruation, but instead the development of breasts. Some Romans believed that menstrual blood had magical powers, that it could cure diseases and that agricultural fertility increased if a menstruating woman ritually walked the fields.

Mature women were thought to be both wetter and softer than men and that they absorbed more liquid in their diets and less physical lifestyle. The buildup of excess fluid in the woman's body was evacuated during the monthly cycle, menstruation. As they aged, it was assumed that women just "dried up," thus ending the need to relieve themselves of excess fluid in menstruation, resulting in menopause. Yes, physically our bodies may crave moisture as we age, but we certainly do not "dry up" in body, spirit, or outlook. Menopause connotes an end of one phase of our lives and the beginning of another, one that can be both rewarding and exciting.

Older women were often seen as wise women in antiquity. The Sibyl of Cumae, for example, was usually portrayed as an old woman who spoke very wise words. Wisdom and old age were valued in Rome; in fact, mental ability was seen as a function of the aging process.

It seems that everywhere we turn today, we confront the stereotypic youthful models daily paraded across the TV screen or staring at us from magazines. Though these are young, vibrant, and beautiful faces, are these the faces of wise women, those whose years of learning and living reflect intelligence and understanding? It is the wise women, the crones, the older women who retain their knowledge and share the wisdom that we must honor and value throughout the year. We are only reminded of their inherent worth in November, when Mother Nature herself shows a few frosty white hairs.

Learn to accept the aging process and, for sure, learn to enjoy life in the autumn. The aging process is sacred, but can be very playful in spirit.

MODERN RITUAL TO HONOR AGING

The older woman is respected in many cultures as the wise woman, the one to be revered whose advice and opinion is sought out by younger women. With the emphasis on youth in our own culture, this vital dimension of the older woman is often disregarded and ignored. As we each age, we must be mindful of the gifts that an older woman can offer. She can counsel with sage advice, she can lead and guide, and she can teach many of life's lessons. It is equally important for the older woman herself, the crone, to feel valued, appreciated and powerful.

Hold up a mirror and look closely at your face. Take your time, and take a careful look. Come to see the inner strength that you possess. Acknowledge your wisdom, your love and your beauty. You have earned this respect, from others and from yourself.

The Agony of Struggle

The word "agony" connotes extreme pain and long suffering; mortal agony is the futile struggle that comes before death. The word agony stems from the ancient Greek word meaning "struggle." The Greek word, however, also contained the sense of competition at philosophical debates, public issues, beauty contests, literary and musical events, and especially the athletic games. These contests pitting rival against rival were called *agones*—fights or struggles for supremacy, for survival and conquest. The most ancient *agones* were sacred competitions following funerals, especially of heroes or leaders, as Homer describes in the *Iliad* to honor the death of Patrocles, friend of Achilles.

November 4–17, I Nones–XIV Kalends December

PLEBEIAN GAMES

The Plebeian Games, or "Games of the People," were held in Rome. They were first mentioned in 216 B.C.E. and firmly established as an annual event by 220 B.C.E. The central event was the Feast of Jupiter on November 15, or the Ides.

Funeral games following religious services at the grave site were customarily held by the Etruscans, the early settlers of the Tuscany region of Italy, who passed on the custom to the Romans. Contest and rivalry for the prize in such events as the foot race, boxing, wrestling, long jump, javelin throwing, and chariot racing may have been a way to express and channel the strong emotions of anger, rage, and grief among the friends of the deceased. Though the origin of the games, the "*Agones*," or Ludi as the Romans called them, was funereal, they grew in size and popularity as Rome itself grew. Annual games to honor deceased heroes were instituted and even added to the religious calendars combining athletic events with competitions in poetry, drama, and music. Eventually, games were established to celebrate events not associated with a funeral, yet they always maintained their religious character, including sacrifice to a deity. During November, the Plebeian Games, the "Games of the People," offered Roman citizens two weeks of clever theatrical presentations juxtaposed with athletic competition. These games were a tribute to the best minds and bodies of the times; they were a religious ritual in November.

The Games of the People were established in the third century B.C.E. and held for several weeks in the first part of November. They marked the second most popular and impressive games held during the Roman year, the first being the Roman Games in September. The focal point of these games was the Feast of Jupiter, held on the Ides.

The first week, November 4–12, was set aside for theatrical and scenic performances. The last three days, November 15–17, were given over to the athletic games held in the Circus Maximus. The two-week event began with a solemn procession led by Rome's magistrates and high priests from the Capitol through the Forum along the Sacred Way to the Circus Maximus.

The eight days of theatrical events were a busy time for art patrons in ancient Rome. Plays, both drama and comedy, were important aspects of Roman religion. A number of religious rites that we have already discussed were always accompanied by games: the festival of Dea Dia in May, Magna Mater in April, Apollo in July, and Jupiter in September. Both the Greeks and Etruscans held funereal games in honor of the deceased, while the regular Greek games such as those held every four years at Olympia (actually there were four or more pan-Hellenic games) were in honor of a deity. At the New Age, or *saeculum,* of Augustus in 17 B.C.E., very special Saecular Games were only part of the ritual for the New Order of Ages and the millennium.

November 13, IDES

JUPITER

The Feast of Jupiter was held on November 13, marking a transition point in the Games of the People from the theatrical to the athletic. There was a solemn rite to Jupiter and a banquet.

November 13, IDES

FERONIA

Feronia is a most ancient goddess associated with agriculture, for she received the firstfruits as her offering. Feronia was especially popular throughout central Italy, yet she also had a sacred grove and temple in Rome. Feronia was also seen as a patroness of freed slaves, the "Goddess of Freedom" she was called. An inscription on her temple at Terracina, where slaves were freed and given the symbolic cap of the freedman, read, "Let the deserving sit down as slaves and rise as freemen."

November 13, IDES

PIETAS

Pietas was a goddess who embodied the quality of respect and duty to the gods, Rome, and one's parents. The quality of devotion exemplified by a child's piety and respect for the mother or father was honored by the Romans. Pietas was depicted as a young women often accompanied by a stork representing the loyalty of child to parent. Pietas warns us to be dutiful to parents, country, and the gods.

For many of us, November is the month of football—either piling on warm clothes, grabbing a thermos of hot coffee, and joining the throng on the bleachers or collapsing in a chair in front of the TV. What else is there to watch over Thanksgiving? For the Romans, November was an equally frenetic sports month in which athletes paraded their finely honed skills before crowds of cheering, avid fans shouting on their favorite team or champion. One difference is that the ancient Roman athletes performed before the gods and goddesses. Sports was a component of the religious ritual—the Ludi dedicated in November to Jupiter.

An ancient author, Dionysus of Halicarnassus (7.72), leaves us a colorful description of the parade and the athletic games. Young men, most likely of leading Roman families, led the procession, riding horseback or driving two- or four-horse chariots. Then came the competing athletes attired only in loincloths. Groups of dancers with flute and lyre players passed by next in the procession. These dancers wore red tunics with bronze belts, crested helmets, and swords and carried short spears. Behind them came other men dressed in goatskins playing the role of satyr and mimicking the warrior dancers. More groups of musicians and dancers followed, together with individuals carrying burning incense and sacred gold or silver ritual urns.

Images of the gods were then carried in procession, including the twelve Olympians as well as Saturn, Ops, Themis, the Muses, the Graces, and the semidivine Hercules, Aesculapius, and others. Finally came the sacrificial animals. The Roman magistrates, serving as priests, officiated over the sacrifice of oxen; then the games would begin.

The events in the Circus Maximus, which could hold 150,000 people, were well attended and began with four-, three-, and two-horse chariot races. In one race, the driver had a companion riding in the chariot; as it crossed the finish line, the companion would leap from the chariot and run the track himself, competing against the other runners to win the whole race. The chariots raced for seven laps around the Circus Maximus, which is equivalent to about five miles and less than fifteen minutes. Then came boxing and wrestling matches, with the winners receiving crowns.

To the ancient Greeks and Romans, athletic skill was a gift of the gods and athletic competition was a form of worship that was taken very seriously—sport and religion were united. Athletes at the Olympic Games in

Greece traditionally offered sacrifice and prayer to Zeus/Jupiter before the events, swearing an oath against cheating, which was on par with blasphemy. It was the priest who gave the signal to start the race, while the victor officiated at the sacrifice to the god. When athletes trained hard and performed well at the games, they were hailed as heroes endowed with a divine blessing—a strong, fit body. The gods and goddesses attended the games and enjoyed a good rivalry and athletic competition; their images were carried in a parade through Rome just behind the athletes. Who could ask for better fan support?

Athletic skill is a wonderful gift. In classical thought, it was as important to develop the body as the mind, so that there was a balance between the two. Our bodies are indeed expressions of the divine. Sacred games and sports under the auspices of the gods and goddesses were the ultimate tribute to the sanctity of the body. The combination of physical dexterity, strength, determination, and drive with hard work and hours of training shows itself in the moments of competition, whatever the sport. Those moments when the runner crosses the finish line, the charioteer pulls ahead of the rest, the wide receiver catches the touchdown pass, the striker puts the soccer ball in the net—those glorious few moments of achievement are moments of euphoria and awe. For the Greeks and Romans, these were sacred moments when the gods gave approving nods.

We honor the spirits in November by turning our attention to the passing of time and in doing so acknowledge the essential human spirit with all its frailties. Yes, we grow old, and in November we accept the process of aging. We revel in the peak moments of human achievements in art and sport, for the mind and the body. We lay back and observe the passing of the month and the end of the year. It is all good. And, most important, it will come again, with subsequent years, new playwrights, new athletes striving to surpass the current records.

MODERN RITUAL FOR COMPETITION, THE AGONY OF THE STRUGGLE

For many women especially, confrontation through direct competition is uncomfortable and best avoided. We too quickly repress our drive to win, our aggressive and competitive side. Yet, in antiquity, there were models of competitive women who were honored and esteemed for their physical prowess. In myth, Atalanta wrestled, hunted, and required her suitors to compete against her in a foot race. In the classical world, we learn from inscriptions that "eleven priestesses of Bacchus put on a running competition," "Tatia directed a gymnasium for women," "My lovely sister Nikegora won the girl's race," and "Kyniska won the chariot race." Every four years, at Olympia, sixteen women together with female assistants put on the games to the goddess Hera, the Heraia. "Here is the method of running. The young women let down their hair, allow their tunic to reach just above the knee, and uncover their right shoulders as far as the breast" (Pausanius 5.16.2–3). They then race through the Olympic stadium. The victorious women received statues with their names inscribed and wreaths of olive leaves.

Support for women's sports is growing with more girls actively participating. Not only can we encourage our daughters to compete, but we also can look for ways to express our competitive side and acknowledge our aggressive and assertive nature. We too can feel the struggle to achieve, the rush at winning, and the agony of defeat, which on a lesser scale parallels the mortal *agones*, the cosmic struggle of life and death.

The cold winter months are upon us now. It is the season when "icicles frozen by bitter winds hang down." (Ovid Metamorphoses *I.201)*

DECEMBER

THE MONTH TO HOPE

Winter nourishes the seed sown in the ploughed earth each year; all is wet with the rains sent by Jupiter. Now, let December bring again the golden festival of Saturn. (Calendar of Filocalus, Degrassi 245)

Rural Menologia

SUN IN SAGITTARIUS

31 DAYS

NONES: DECEMBER 5

DAYLIGHT: 9 HOURS

DARKNESS: 15 HOURS

SOLSTICE

Farmers were advised to manure the fields, sow beans and gather olives, dig new ditches, clear old ditches, clear vineyards, prune trees in orchards, and plant lilies and crocuses. (Menologia)

We come full circle now, to December, the final month in our year. Twelve months ago, we began this spiritual voyage. We journeyed together to a world where time does not tick away by minutes and hours, but instead moves in a steady cyclical progression through the natural world and the seasons, with the recurring phases of birth, life, death, and rebirth. We moved through the sacred seasonal landscape from the dark, shivering cold of January into the sap-raising, sensual spring months, through the heat of fullness and ripeness in summer to the end, the decline and loss of autumn. We opened ourselves on the deepest level to be strengthened and healed. We returned to the world of nature, where the gods and goddesses, the water sprites and woodland nymphs reside. The yearlong path took us to strange and mysterious places—a soulful journey following the path of the sun itself. We moved forward from the first month after the winter solstice to the longest days of summer; from the declining daylight of autumn to the shortest day of the year in December. Now, we return to the days of the winter solstice and the deities worshiped this December month.

In the oldest Roman calendars, those based upon the lunar cycle, March was the first month of the new year and December the tenth and last. In fact, the Latin word for ten, *decem,* names this as the tenth month—the period of gestation for a human child according to the lunar calendar. While March and Mars are synonymous with male fertility and conception, December is the month of birth. This association of birth and December is not a unique concept; Christians view December 25 as the birth of the baby Jesus, and the sun itself is reborn at the solstice of December 21.

The Saturnalia, the weeklong rite to the god Saturn dominates the rituals for December. In the words of the Roman poet Catullus, of the first century B.C.E., this period in mid-December was the "best of days." The Saturnalia was not the distorted caricature of ancient Romans rushing from one orgy to the next, drinking, gambling, partying, enjoying unrestrained sex, and honoring a pagan rite devoid of spiritual meaning. The god Saturn was honored at the winter solstice beginning with public ritual involving both sacrifice and a grand banquet held at the impressive temple of Saturn in Rome. The Saturnalia was a festive time that lasted for seven days in mid-December with private parties, special dinners, family celebrations, and the exchange of gifts. In fact, small dolls and candles with candle holders were traditional Saturnalia gifts. This festival, one of the most popular in ancient Rome, was celebrated into the third and fourth centuries C.E., with many of its customs being incorporated in the Christian holiday of Christmas.

Saturn is a complex god worshiped in the oldest days of Rome as an earthbound deity of sowing and seeds. His very name was derived from the Latin word for "sowing" and "seed," *satus*. Saturn was the god who taught people how to cultivate the earth and to plant the seed in the moist soil. We still honor this god by referring to the holy day of Saturn as Saturday. Saturn was King of All during the Golden Age, a most ancient time long before his son Jupiter took command. Every December, he was remembered and honored by the Romans as wise ruler of the Golden Age.

The Rule of Saturn: The Golden Age

The first age was the Golden Age, an age without warriors or conquerors. Everyone kept faith and pursued the right path on their own; they needed no laws to tell them what to do. There was no fear of punishment, no crimes, no jails. There were no lawyers, no judges, and no one coming before a magistrate to plead a case. All lived free, yet without the need of law.

The tree had never been chopped down, felled, or removed from its natural place on the mountainside; its wood was not sold for profit and shipped to foreign ports. Just like the trees, people also remained safe on their own land and shores. Cities were not circled by steep trenches and walls for defense. There were no war trumpets, no war horns of curving brass, no swords, no helmets. There was no need for armed men. All the countries, safe from war, passed the years in peace and prosperity.

In the Golden Age, the Earth herself, without being forced or abused, was not touched by plough or hoe. On her own, Earth gave all the things humans need. And mortals were content with the food that came easily: gathered fruits, strawberries from the mountainsides, cherries and berries hanging thick on prickly branches, nuts fallen from the spreading boughs of Jupiter's tree, the oak.

The spring lasted forever. Gentle breezes with warm breath played with the flowers that grew unplanted. The Earth, untilled, brought forth her vast stores of grain, and the fields, always fertile, grew white with the heavy stalks of ripened grain. Streams of milk, and streams of sweet nectar flowed; and yellow honey was gathered from hives in the green oak tree. (Ovid *Metamorphoses* 1.89–111)

Ovid speaks of the four ages of human habitation on the earth, the Golden, the Silver, the Bronze, and the fourth and final, the Age of Iron, in which we live today. The Golden Age was the time of Saturn, Ruler of the World. This was an idyllic time with no war, strife, or want. Food was readily available, the gods and goddesses inhabited the earth, and all was well. Transition to the Age of Silver occurred when Jupiter overthrew Saturn.

During the Age of Silver, time was partitioned into seasons of spring, summer, fall, and winter. In this age, people were forced to find shelter in houses, whereas during the Golden Age they had lived in caves and forest homes. This was the age that saw cultivation of grain and domestication of animals, who "groaned beneath the heavy yoke." The Age of Bronze followed, a sterner time when fighting and war existed, yet impiety toward the gods did not.

The Iron Age, the last, was the final descent from the Golden Age. "All evil burst forth. Modesty, truth, and faith fled the Earth, and in their place came tricks, deceit, violence, and the cursed love of gain." Men traveled across the known world, cutting down the trees to make boats. Now, the earth itself was divided and partitioned by the surveyor, sold as property to the highest bidder. Humans were greedy and, seeking more gain, they delved into the earth itself, mining for the wealth that the Creatrix had hidden away. This wealth of gold and silver only provoked humans to crime. War came, and weapons of iron. Men lived on plunder, and guests were not safe from the host. Husbands and wives hated each other and sought an end to marriage. "Piety to the gods and goddesses lay vanquished, and the maiden Astraea, the last of the immortals, abandoned the blood-soaked Earth." Astraea, you see, was the Goddess of Justice. She was the last to leave, as she could no longer look on the wickedness of humankind.

The concept of an idyllic era in the history of humankind is compelling. The ancient Romans did believe in the Golden Age, and they held to a tradition that the Golden Age could be restored and the gods and goddesses would one day return. The Roman author Virgil tells us it will be when the Cumaean Sibyl has brought us to the end of the millennium. The advent of the new millennium celebrated in 17 B.C.E. with great games and ritual would be a New Age—a new *saeculum*—ushering in a New Order of the Ages.

The Golden Age vividly expresses an ideal human world without crime, without the violence or aggression of one human against another. A Golden Age has no suffering, and all are fed and nourished. All live in communion with nature, and the natural world bestows blessings upon the race of humankind. This is a world where greed, gain, and material worth are not idolized. This is a world in which the environment is not only respected, but held in awe. This is a world in which nature, manifest as the gods and goddesses, nymphs and satyrs, was worshiped.

Today we seem to be closer to the Iron Age. Memory of the Golden Age has vanished. Yet for a few days in December, we are reminded of those divine days, when there was peace and prosperity before the goddesses and gods withdrew. December's legacy is the revival of those cherished memories—the good, the plentiful, and the "best of days." In December, we incorporate those values and dare to dream of a Golden Age. This too is a religious act.

RITES AND RITUALS OF DECEMBER

The Good

Good things begin to happen with the Good Goddess, Bona Dea. In December, just before the winter solstice when the sun's progression into darkness is complete, Roman women gathered together in the private house of the appointed priestess, a woman of unblemished virtue. They gathered on this dark winter night to celebrate a mystery rite to a goddess whose name was so secret that we know her only as the Good Goddess, or Bona Dea. Her real name was never stated publicly.

December 3, III Nones

B O N A   D E A

Bona Dea, also known as Damia (Da Mater or Demeter), was an earth goddess who promoted fertility in women. Her rites were secret, as was her true name. The woman officiating as her priestess during the ritual was called Damiatrix.

A play, music, and sacred objects revealed only to attendees were part of the ritual. The room for the service was decorated with vine leaves, a pig was offered, and wine that was named "milk" was offered to Bona Dea and then drunk by the worshipers.

This rite to the Good Goddess was considered of a private nature as it took place not in a temple, but in the home of the consul, whose wife served as priestess. The public rite at the temple of Bona Dea was held on May 1. In contrast, the December ritual was not paid for at state expense and the high priest did not attend; nor, however, did any males, for this was strictly a female ritual.

The rites were desecrated in 62 B.C.E., when Clodius, dressing as a woman, attended the rites at the house of Julius Caesar, whose mother, Aurelia, and wife, Pompeia, presided. Aurelia recognized Clodius and ended the rites, quickly covering up the sacred objects that were forbidden to male view. When the sacrilege was discovered, Clodius was driven from the house and the Vestal Virgins began the rites again. Regardless, Caesar divorced his wife on these grounds, saying that the wife of Caesar had to be above suspicion.

Mystery rites for women only, involving sacred objects displayed only to women, held in a private house where all pictures of men are covered with veils . . . Just what went on in that house where the room was decorated with vine leaves and wine was renamed "mother's milk" and drunk?

Music, plays, and dancing for women only? The men were very suspicious, curious, and perhaps a little jealous or fearful, for nothing seems to threaten and intrigue men more than deep, dark female secrets. Clodius sneaks in, Cicero wants to know the exact date and location, and Juvenal, a Roman satirist, wrote a ridiculous description of the Bona Dea rite, even though he never attended. He assumes that when women share ritual alone in a private house for the Good Goddess, their central theme must be sexual exploitation of men. Wild women can never trusted!

> *The secret rites of the Good Goddess*
> *are pretty well known,*
> *When a flute stirs their loins and*
> *the Maenads of Priapus groan*
> *And howl in frenzy from music and*
> *wine and toss their hair.*
> *Oh, how they burn for intercourse,*
> *what cries declare their throbbing lust . . .*
> *They're females without inhibitions and*
> *around the ritual den*
> *Rings a cry from every corner:*
> *"We're ready! Bring in the men!"*
>
> (Juvenal 6.314 ff.)

MODERN RITUAL TO WILD WOMEN AND THE GOOD GODDESS, BONA DEA

Women's personal time together and women's private rites will always remain a mystery to men. Gather with your women friends to perform a ritual to the wild side, that part of your being that identifies with the holiest goddess, She Who Can Never Be Named. Offer her some wine, drink in some "mother's milk," and share secrets with women friends. We can all use a beneficent nod from the Good Goddess, Bona Dea.

The Kind and Plentiful

On this day in December, the *pagani*, the country people and farmers, called upon Faunus, beneficial Spirit of the Wild, the Kindly One, to bless the countryside and farms. On this joyful holiday, worshipers offered wine and sacrifice on smoking altars of earth throughout the countryside and danced wildly in the fields that they at other times worked so hard.

December 5, NONES

FAUNUS

HYMN TO FAUNUS

O Faunus, you who love to chase the fleet-footed nymphs,

With kind intentions, may you walk the boundaries of my farm and cross over my sunny meadows.

Guarantee me a fertile and bountiful year, and I will not fail in pouring a libation of wine to you.

You, O friend of Venus, Goddess of the Garden, may the ancient altars smoke with incense in your honor.

The flocks roam the grassy fields when December 5 comes around.

The country people put on their festive clothes to celebrate your holiday.

The wolf walks among the lambs that are not afraid.

In your honor, Faunus, the forest sheds its foliage.

The valley resonates with the beat of music and dancing feet in your honor.

(Horace *Odes* 3.18)

December rituals celebrated the plentiful bounty, with Consus, the God of the Store Bin, and Ops, the Goddess of Plenty, honored this month. The "good life," the life of plenty, when the wolf walks among the lambs that are not fearful—these ideal qualities are honored by ritual in December.

―――――――――――――――――――――――――――――――――――――

December 13, IDES

TELLUS AND CERES

The temple to Tellus was dedicated on the Ides of December. The Senate met here on occasion and a large map of Italy was painted on its walls. Ceres was also honored on these Ides with a banquet.

―――――――――――――――――――――――――――――――――――――

December 15, XVI KALENDS JANUARY

CONSUS

CONSUALIA

December 15 marks another festival to Consus, together with chariot races and games.

―――――――――――――――――――――――――――――――――――――

December 19, XII KALENDS JANUARY

OPS

OPALIA

The goddess Ops was honored in the midst of the Saturnalia.

―――――――――――――――――――――――――――――――――――――

"The Best of Days, Io Saturnalia!"

December is a cold dark month; its short period of daylight is overshadowed by the many hours of relentless dark. December is the month of the winter solstice and of transition, for the solstice marks a turning point in the course of the sun. In December, the sun reverses its course and the solar journey starts afresh toward longer hours of sunlight and decreasing hours of night. December is a pivotal month, marking the distinction between two very different solar paths. Different worlds and different paths is a theme of the December rituals to Saturn.

December 17–23, XIV–VIII KALENDS JANUARY

SATURN

SATURNALIA

The Saturnalia festivities opened at the temple of Saturn with a sacrifice to the god, followed by a lavish banquet. At the sacrifice and offering, the Romans wore their best clothes (togas required), yet they changed for the banquet into more casual, comfortable clothes and soft woolen caps. The banquet ended with a communal shout of "Io Saturnalia." Then came a week or more of parties, dinners, and social events. Shops were closed, official business stopped, and everyone celebrated the Saturnalia. Public gambling, drinking, and partying were condoned. The Roman author Pliny complained of the noise and shut himself up in a soundproof room while the rest of the household celebrated.

Yet for one ancient author and for most Romans, "It was the best of days."

This was a special time in the home when roles were reversed and masters waited upon their slaves. A "king of Saturnalia" was chosen in the household, and gifts were exchanged, including the traditional ceramic doll figures for children and wax candles for friends. Extra wine and food were set out for slave and master each night. The Saturnalia itself was celebrated into the fifth century C.E.

The weeklong Saturnalia, the ritual to Saturn, highlights differences and opposites, focusing on the master and the slave, the bound and unbound, the corrupt and the innocent, the bad and the good, the Age of Iron that we live in and the Age of Gold ruled by Saturn.

December 21, X KALENDS JANUARY

ANGERONA

DIVALIA

The Divalia, in honor of Angerona, was a secret ritual, and another mystery rite—the statue even had her mouth bound shut. This goddess was associated with the disease of angina.

The most famous of Roman holidays, the Saturnalia shares a certain reputation for rowdiness and debauchery. It did have a serious component, not unlike our holiday season in December. We can understand the festive December season, when we put aside our normal daily routine of work and school is suspended. After all, this is the time of year to shop and exchange presents, to buy new holiday outfits, to plan special feasts and gatherings with friends and family, to drink, eat, and make merry. Underneath all the revelry, however, are the very solemn and joyous religious events of Christmas and Hanukkah. The ancient Romans did exactly the same thing in mid-December over two thousand years ago when they celebrated the Saturnalia.

The temple of Saturn was located at the base of the Capitol and dedicated on December 17. Standing inside was a statue of the god that was filled with oil and also bound with woolen binds. During his December ritual these were undone, and Saturn was freed. One ancient author suggests that this was similar to the seed or the human embryo, bound in the mother's womb and bursting free in the tenth month. Thus, December would be the month the babe was born. Recall that the most ancient calendars began in March, hence December was, as the name states, the tenth month originally.

December 23, VIII KALENDS JANUARY

LARENTINA

LARENTALIA

This ritual involved the performance of funeral rites before the tomb of the goddess Larentina. Here priests made offering to the Di Manes. Larentina may have been the mother of the Lares, the protective deities of Rome, yet her background is uncertain.

December 25, VI KALENDS JANUARY

SOL INVICTUS

BRUMA

This day was made sacred to Sol Invictus in 273 C.E., though before that it had little significance. The ancient Romans called it Bruma, or winter solstice, the time when the year passed the shortest day.

A closer look at the Saturnalia suggests a nature-driven theme, when things are turned upside down and worlds are reversed for just a few days; for this is when the sun reverses its course and, having passed the shortest day, now begins to move toward the longest. In December it is appropriate to ritually switch things around a little bit. The Saturnalia represents in one respect an "inversion ritual." For a limited time and within the context of a controlled religious rite, reality is altered and roles are reversed. The slave sat at the table and was waited on by the master, gambling was permitted in public when it was forbidden throughout the year, and informal clothes were worn for dinner instead of the formal toga. The hat of freedom, a felt cap called a *pilleus* worn by freed slaves, was worn by all people; a "Lord of Misrule" was chosen within each household to rule over the festivities; and slaves would wear their masters' clothes.

This ritualized role reversal served a deeper purpose in breaking up, for just a few days, the established hierarchy and exposing the artificiality of customary fixed roles within a household—roles defined by societal expectation. The Saturnalia ritual, performed with mockery and jest, in fact provided a chance for greater compassion and empathy between master and slave. The ritual itself could lead to a loosening of expectations and perhaps an increased tolerance of those living under the same-roofed atrium.

Compassion and tolerance for other family members are qualities we all can strive for, especially during this holiday season. How easy it is to become locked into demanding and fixed roles within a household. "Mom, make me a sandwich!" "Is my new shirt clean for school?" "Pick me up at the station tonight." "I need some money." Cook, cleaner, chauffeur, nurturer, and general all-around provider is a role that falls to many women. Yet roles and expectations between family members can become unflinching and oppressive for everyone, eventually becoming a source of great anger. This month, we need to become conscious of those roles within our own family or among our friends. We need to determine what is expected of each person and whether we are comfortable with it or would prefer a change. Perhaps a change is due. December is the month for reversal.

MODERN INVERSION RITUAL

December is a pivotal month when the sun reverses its course. We honor the reversal and the inversion theme through our customary rituals of December when we put aside our regular routines of work or school to celebrate the December holidays or we bring a tree growing wild in nature indoors to decorate with mementos and tokens. Follow nature's lesson, this season, and carry on this ancient Roman custom of inversion with your family, friends, or community. Identify the roles played by each family member and reverse them for fun, just for a few days around the time of the solstice. Have the children make decisions normally relegated to adults. Switch the household jobs or seating arrangements at the dining room table. Shake things up a bit! Do the unexpected! These small acts recall the spirit of the Saturnalia and are of religious significance, connecting directly with the natural world.

We look forward to this time of joy and anticipate a festive atmosphere when our lives change for just a little bit. Spiritually, we also seek a reconnection with the divine spirit. Gift giving then as now was a popular expression of friendship, love, and harmony. Along with the traditional gifts of candles and dolls, a variety of objects were purchased and exchanged between friends and family. In large families, presents were drawn blindfolded for gift exchange, much like today's "Secret Santa." You can imagine the crowded streets in ancient Rome, full of men, women, and children rushing from shop to shop, searching for the perfect gift at the jewelers, the perfumers store, the leather shop, or the clothing store. People pushed and crowded into the wine dealers, the grocers, the pastry shops to buy the extra amphora of Falernian wine and the necessary ingredients for those special Saturnalia recipes.

THE RITE OF GIFT GIVING, SMALL OFFERINGS TO OUR LOVED ONES

As for modern ritual, we already celebrate in December much as the ancient Romans did. The week surrounding the winter solstice is a time for celebration, gift giving, and also religious ritual. The darkest days call for celebration of the return of the light and the magical birth.

The Roman author Martial, who lived in the first century C.E., published two collections of sayings. Each came out in December, the *Xenia* in 83 C.E. and the *Apophoreta* in 85 C.E., and were meant to be of practical use during the Saturnalia. They were collections of clever two-line messages designed to accompany gifts given at the Saturnalia. Readers could then choose the saying that was most appropriate for their gift. The idea of Christmas cards and modern greeting cards is not new!

*Gift Ideas for the Saturnalia Season
of 83 C.E., by Martial, with Seasonal Message*

Ivory writing tablet (ideal for those over forty years of age): "If wax tablets are too dim for your failing eyes, Paint this new white ivory tablet with large black letters!" (*Apophoreta* 5)

Small writing tablets (for love letters or billing clients): "Because we are small, you may think that we are only used to write love letters. You're wrong! We can demand money as well." (9)

Letter paper: "Whether sent to a slight acquaintance or someone close, this paper will address everyone as 'Dear Friend.'" (11)

Wooden cashbox: "If you find anything in the bottom of this box, then it will be your present. Is there nothing? Then the box itself is your present." (13)

Case for writing materials: "So now that you have received this writing case, remember to fill it with pens. I have given you the larger case, you must furnish the lesser items." (20)

Gold hair pin: "So that your just washed wet hair will not ruin your silk hair bands. Let a gold pin fix and hold up your curly locks." (24)

Umbrella: "Accept a sunshade to fight off rays of the fierce sun. If there is wind or rain, this will cover you too." (28)

Bedroom lamp: "I am a lamp, confidante of your sweet bed. Do whatever you wish, I won't tell." (39)

Hand weights/dumbbells: "Why do your strong arms go to waste on these silly dumbbells? Get outside and dig a vineyard—this is better exercise for men." (49)

Baby rattle: "If a baby clings to your neck, weeping, let him shake this noisy rattle with his small hand." (54)

Toothpaste: "Don't give me to an older person. Give me to a young girl. I'm not in the habit of polishing false teeth bought at the store." (56)

Leather breast band/bra: "This small leather skin may not be large enough for your breasts. You may need an entire bull's hide." (66)

Strainer for snow (a metal colander held over a wine goblet in which a lump of snow was placed and wine strained through to chill it): "Take my advice, only use expensive wine with my snow. Anything cheaper will only stain your napkins." (103)

A Modern Celebration

The Saturnalia of ancient Rome was a time to feast, much as Christmas is in Italy today. The feasts, the games, the gift giving, the music, and the religious rituals are all very much part of the December festival season in modern Rome, much as they were in antiquity. This has not changed in over two thousand years.

MODERN RITUAL: FOODS FOR SATURNALIA

Here are some traditional Saturnalia recipes prepared by the women of ancient Rome. Enjoy them this festival season.

HONEYED DATES *(serves 10)*

"Pit the dates and stuff them with walnuts or even pine nuts. . . . Roll them in a little salt and fry them with honey. Serve." (Apicius 7.13.1)

1 pound dried dates	salt, as needed
walnuts, 1 for each date	honey, as needed

Use good-quality dates (they should not be sticky and the skins should not come off easily). Pit them by making a cut on one side. Fill each cavity with a walnut. Roll them lightly in salt and cook them in honey in a skillet until they are caramelized. As soon as the dates are carmelized, put them on a lightly oiled plate to prevent sticking. Serve. (Apicius *De Re Coquinaria* VII.13.1)

GLOBI

8 ounces ricotta cheese	1 large egg
1/2 cup semolina flour	1/4 teaspoon salt

Mix ricotta with the semolina in a medium-sized bowl. Beat the egg and stir into the mixture. Add salt and mix well.

Pour enough oil in a pan to cover the Globi, about an inch, and heat the oil. Drop the dough in teaspoonfuls into the heated oil, and fry until brown. Remove and drain well on a paper towel. Dip in honey and serve. Globi can also be dipped in salsa or other sauces.

December's rituals bring promise. For Christians it is the promise of salvation and a better life with the birth of the Christ Child. For the pagan Romans, it was the promise of the Golden Age and the Rule of Saturn. It is the promise of a spiritual life, a life blessed and in accord with the deities.

Saturn harkens back to the Golden Age, an age of piety. It is for this age we must now hope. At the millennium, we begin the New Order of the Ages. For spiritual guidance, we can learn from the gods and goddess the ancient practices. As Saturn asks, "Who would bring incense to my smoking altars?"

The first age was golden when authority was not needed. Men and women revered justice and virtue. They kept faith. (Ovid Metamorhoses I.90–92)

BIBLIOGRAPHY

Burkert, Walter. *Greek Religion*. Cambridge: Harvard University Press, 1985.

Campbell, Joseph. *The Masks of God: Primitive Mythology*. New York: Penguin, 1958.

Dalby, Andrew, and Sally Grainger. *The Classical Cookbook*. Malibu, CA: J. Paul Getty Museum, 1996.

Donato, Giuseppe, and Monique Seefried. *The Fragrant Past*. Atlanta: Emory University, 1989.

Estés, Clarissa Pinkola. *Women Who Run with the Wolves*. New York: Ballantine, 1992.

Field, Carol. *Celebrating Italy*. New York: Harper Perennial, 1990.

Hanh, Thich Nhat. *Peace Is Every Step: The Path of Mindfulness in Everyday Life*. New York: Bantam, 1991.

McDowell, Christopher, and Tricia Clark-McDowell. *The Sanctuary Garden*. New York: Simon & Schuster, 1998.

Murray, Elizabeth. *Cultivating Sacred Space: Gardening for the Soul*. Rohnert Park, CA: Pomegranate, 1997.

Rich, Adrienne. *Of Woman Born: Motherhood as Experience and Institution*. New York: Norton, 1976.

Ricotti, Eugenia Salza Prina. *Dining as a Roman Emperor*. Rome: L'Erma di Bretschneider, 1968.

Scullard, H. H. *Festivals and Ceremonies of the Roman Republic*. Ithaca: Cornell Thames & Hudson, 1981.

Seth, K., ed. *Pyramid Texts*. 1908.

Starhawk. *The Spiral Dance*. San Francisco: HarperSanFrancisco, 1979.

ANCIENT SOURCES

All translations of myths and other ancient texts are by the author unless noted.

Apuleius. *The Golden Ass.* Trans. Jack Lindsay. Indiana: Indiana University Press, 1960.

Cato. *De Agricultura.* From Naphtali Lewis and Meyer Reinhold. *Roman Civilization Sourcebook* I. New York: Harper and Row, 1951.

Corpus Inscriptionum Latinarum. Berlin: 1863.

Degrassi, A. *Inscriptiones Italiae.* Rome: XIII.3.

Juvenal. *The Satires of Juvenal.* Trans. Hubert Creekmore. New York: Mentor Classic, 1963.

Ovid. *Fasti.* Trans. James Fraser. Loeb Classical Library (LCL). Cambridge: Harvard University Press, 1931.

Ovid. *Metamorphoses.* Trans. Frank Miller. Loeb Classical Library (LCL). Cambridge: Harvard University Press, 1911.

Theocritus. *Idyll 15.* Andrew Lang, *Theocritus, Bion, and Moschus.* London: MacMillan and Co., 1911.

Virgil. *The Aeneid.* Trans. David West. London: Penguin, 1991.

INDEX